FROM LEARNING TO EARNING 2002

How to **maximise** your future employability by choosing the **right degree**

Nick Higgins
&
Cliff Pettifor

TROTMAN

From Learning to Earning 2002

This first edition published in 2002 by Trotman and Company Ltd
2 The Green, Richmond, Surrey TW9 1PL

The quotations in Chapter 3 and research in Chapter 6 were reproduced from DfES-CSU-AGCAS-IER *Moving On – Graduate Careers Three Years after Graduation 1999* thanks to kind permission from the publishers CSU Limited and the report's authors Kate Purcell, Professor of Employment Studies at Bristol Business School, and Peter Elias, Professor at the Institute for Employment Research, Warwick University.

British Library Cataloguing in Publication Data
A catalogue record for this book is available from the British Library

ISBN 0 85660 817 3

Design/layout Robin Mills
Typeset by Palimpsest Book Production Limited,
Polmont, Stirlingshire
Printed and bound in Great Britain by Bell & Bain Ltd

contents

ACKNOWLEDGEMENTS

Thank you to past and present colleagues at *Harlaxton College* and the many employers without whose support and ideas these surveys would be impossible.

Thank you also to Amanda Williams at *Trotman Publishing*, Andrew Bottomley at *PricewaterhouseCoopers*, Richard Illingworth at the *Audit Commission*, Kate Purcell, Peter Elias and everyone who was kind enough to provide much appreciated advice, support and assistance.

This book is dedicated to the *secret seven* . . . they know who they are!

ABOUT THE AUTHORS

Nick Higgins graduated in Economics from Cambridge University in 1998. After a short break spent 'developing his employment skills' he joined Trotman Publishing. The time since has seen him research, write and edit over 30 careers and educational guides and one award-winning website.

Today, he is Trotman's full-time in-house writer/researcher, working on many new and exciting projects.

● ●

Cliff Pettifor enjoyed 20 years of industrial experience in textiles and clothing, from the extremes of door-to-door selling to sales management. After graduating as a mature student from the Nottingham Trent University, he completed a PhD in 'The Economics of Higher Education' in 1984, before focusing his research on the causes and effects of university reputations.

He currently teaches for the Open University and for Harlaxton College, the British Campus of the University of Evansville, Indiana, from where he directs the Performance Indicator Project (PIP) and the annual Graduate Recruiters' Surveys.

FOREWORD

Donald MacLeod, Higher Education Executive Editor for the Guardian, *reflects on higher education's eternal conflict – that of academia vs. employability.*

A degree is for life – not just getting that first job. For many academics, introducing their students to the delights of their beloved subject comes a long way ahead of fitting them for a particular job. A student's employment prospects are not necessarily their concern. They are there to teach young people to think, to open their minds to the best and most recent of what has been thought and written. For the academic, knowledge is worthwhile for its own sake.

But unless there is a decent job – or indeed an entire career – at the end of the course any graduate is going to feel short-changed – all that study, and nowadays all that debt, in return for unemployment or years of unsatisfactory work? No thanks! Students – and their parents – expect there to be earning after learning. If 84 per cent of students believe the money they are spending on their education is a good investment, they are surely thinking about their future bank balances as well as simply acquiring a well-stocked mind.

So there is a tension at the heart of the university experience, between what academics want to teach and what students want to learn, and it is one that has been around for some time. In the 19th century people like George Birkbeck – founder of the London college – promoted the idea of 'useful knowledge' and in mechanics' institutes where the students paid for the lectures they insisted on getting the instruction they considered useful – not the Latin the lecturers wanted to teach them.

Today it is not the working class in Britain but great tracts of the developing world that are demanding useful knowledge. Western universities may have thought they would dispense rounded courses of culture and knowledge to a waiting world; but what the world wants is business studies, IT and health-related courses.

For the student trying to make sense of the UK higher education jungle and plot a way through to a job at the end there seems to be a paradox: the more vocational the degree the less likely it is to lead to a top job – for the best start on the career ladder study something really useless! Merchant banks happily recruit theoretical physics graduates, law firms snap up classicists whose legal knowledge probably stops with Cicero but whose brains, honed on translating Homer, are assumed to have the precision required to shred an opponent's case. Meanwhile those who study media studies or something else overtly vocational are sneered at by the former chief inspector for schools as doing 'vacuous Mickey Mouse' degrees. Can a degree in Surf Science be serious? Ask the critics.

Well, that's an exaggeration. But there still exist some employers who are more impressed by the standing of a university and proven ability in a well-established subject, than they are by the efforts of academics to make their courses relevant. However, times are changing and employers are placing increasing emphasis on personal interactive skills. In the old days everyone assumed you learned these skills merely by taking part in sport or organising a society or entertainment at the students union. Now, you need to be able to demonstrate specifically how you have done so.

What modern students almost certainly do – unlike their parents' generation – is hold down a term time job as well as studying. This now becomes a very important part of their CVs.

And yes, a degree in Surf Science is extremely serious, maintains Professor Roderick Floud, president of Universities UK, the representative body for the heads of British universities. The innovative course at Plymouth University has succeeded in packaging together rigorous academic disciplines that include oceanic science, materials technology and business studies, he said. 'These underpin its intellectual validity. And the course is designed to engage with, and appeal to young people who often do not see higher education as relevant to them because it connects with their interests and sparks their imagination. It was launched in response to demand from local employers, enjoys sponsorship from industry and has been franchised in Hawaii and Western Australia. So in this case the pursuit of knowledge "learning for learning's sake" if you like also provides a firm foundation for future employment.'

But can vocational courses really make students think? Professor Floud, a respected economic historian, also defends vocational degrees against the criticism that no subject can be suitable for degree level study unless it has a body of literature and its own methods of investigation in place.

'The experience of the research community shows that many of the new research discoveries have been made at the boundaries of traditional subjects. In the past, new subjects have grown up this way and eventually we have taught them under their new subject headings to undergraduates. Today the whole process is telescoped by the speed of change; research areas translate rapidly into knowledge based industries which need us to provide undergraduate programmes to staff them at graduate level,' he says.

So new and vocational degrees *can* be at the intellectual cutting edge, just as traditional 'academic' degrees *can* lead straight to vocational careers. Clearly, therefore, there is no 'best' degree subject or institution to attend in order to get your dream job or career. The key is to choose the course and university 'best' for you. And you are likely to do your very best, both academically and in terms of future employability, by studying a subject that interests you in an environment you find comfortable and stimulating.

Donald MacLeod
Higher Education Executive Editor, the Guardian

PREFACE

Carl Gilleard, Chief Executive of the Association of Graduate Recruiters, offers the recruiter's view of graduate employability and higher education.

There is no doubt about the growing importance of graduates being adequately prepared for the demands of a fast changing world of work. Government, the education sector, employers and students themselves must work together to ensure that future generations of graduates entering the labour market are fully employable.

But why do employers recruit graduates in the first place? In essence, it is because they believe graduates bring 'added value' to the organisation. Organisations need workers who can learn quickly, reflect on what they have learnt and apply it. Graduates, by studying for a degree, have demonstrated their intellectual ability and, hopefully, a willingness to continue learning throughout their working life.

However, in the 21st century graduates need to offer employers more than academic achievement. Increasingly, employers are seeking graduates who can offer a range of essential skills. Some graduates gain *specialist* skills through their degree courses, but all graduates need to demonstrate the *transferable* skills that employers value so highly – such as teamworking, communication skills and problem solving. Note my use of the word 'demonstrate'. There is little point in possessing skills if you are unable to show that you have them during the recruitment and selection process.

What else do employers look for in graduate recruits? Past work experience is seen as an asset – particularly if it is relevant to your chosen career area. Employers are also beginning to place more importance on graduates being able to manage their own career development – an indication perhaps of the uncertainty of career paths in the future. And it cannot be emphasised enough how much employers value such old fashioned attributes as enthusiasm, motivation, flexibility and adaptability.

All of these qualities are important in securing that all-important first career opening – but it doesn't stop there. Graduate employability can also be defined as 'the ability to get a job, do it well, then get another job, do that well, then another job and so on . . .'

There are those who claim it is unreasonable of employers to have such high expectations, to which I respond that employers who spend vast sums in recruiting and developing graduates want to be as sure as possible that they will get a good return on their investment. Like it or not, it is the way of the world and there is no turning back. The age of the graduate who can 'hit the ground running' is here to stay.

Perhaps the most important step forward in enhancing graduate employability is to make sure you are fully prepared to take advantage of the higher education experience. It should enable you to:

- experiment and explore your potential

- identify and focus on the skills that you are most interested in developing

- understand how these can help you decide where you want to go in life and how to get there

- learn how to take control of your work/life planning.

Teachers, careers advisers and books such as this one can help you make the crucial decision of choosing the right course and university but, once there, the responsibility for getting the most out of being an undergraduate is down to you.

Those of you who do maximise the benefits of the HE experience and take full advantage of what is on offer are the ones who will most easily be able to convince employers that you are worth investing in. Once in work, you can apply the same approach to ensure you remain employable.

Graduate employability is in everyone's best interest – from the graduate whose quality of life will be enhanced, the higher education sector which must demonstrate to future generations that HE is a sound investment and the employer who gets a more rounded and capable employee. That's something we should all strive to achieve. The challenge should not be beyond us if we pull together. After all, the very essence of being a graduate is to fulfil your true potential.

Carl Gilleard
Chief Executive, Association of Graduate Recruiters

INTRODUCTION – A WORD TO THE WISE. . .

Val Butcher, Senior Adviser for Employability with the Generic Centre of the UK LTSN (Learning and Teaching Support Network), examines how From Learning to Earning *relates to the various interested parties.*

. . . Students and their advisers (including family and friends!)

'WARNING: Before reading on, remember this: you should always bear in mind that the ultimate responsibility for your development into a well-rounded and employable graduate lies with you. A university or course, or department or tutor can provide you with the necessary environment and basic tools, but it is you who must use them to your advantage.'

This warning is peppered throughout the book. It is so important that it deserves to be highlighted here. I support entirely the authors' clear wish that nobody reading this volume will be foolish enough to think that the way to become employable is through the simple expedient of gaining a place on a course at a university or college which features highly in the statistical tables for the subject of your choice.

Of course, nobody bright enough to be aiming for a degree course would think it possible that employability can be achieved by no more than making a good or lucky choice of degree . . . Really? I used to work in a Careers Service which offered help to all students from the area who left their higher education courses prematurely, and I have heard it all:

'My teacher said it was a good course when she went there after the war'. 'I really fancied the blokes in the prospectus photographs'. 'My Dad's partner said he'd read an article somewhere that said that there were a lot of jobs for that degree . . .'

A degree course is going to cost you – or your family – a lot of money. Even if you have been working for years before entering higher education, there will be fees and loss of earnings to weigh in the balance. Make the most of it.

Part 1 of this book is packed full of useful and up-to-date ideas for making the most of your higher education experience. Act on this – it will be too late when you are confronted by questions like *'What is the most challenging experience you have had? How did you cope with it?'* on application forms – not only applications for graduate jobs, but also for interesting gap year opportunities after your degree.

There are other messages lurking in these pages which deserve star billing:

Learn how to research opportunities Following the advice here on researching and evaluating the relevant information on universities and courses should only be the start of developing this skill for life. You will need it to navigate the increasing range of options in

your degree programme; to find out exactly what is involved in extra-curricular opportunities; to look behind the glossy recruitment literature and websites about graduate vacancies in your final year. Incredibly, many students do not apply the same time or skill to making a major life decision like a choice of a course or job as they would to writing a geography essay or a physics lab report.

Where can you find information about how far a degree course or institution can offer 'the value-added' employability experiences? Part 1 will alert you to a range of possibilities which you should check out. These will include:

- Opportunities for structured work experience, both in modules and extra curricular.

- Are there Career Development Learning modules? At what level? For whom?

- Are there Entrepreneurship modules or Graduate Enterprise?

There are also a growing number of indicators that the Government is requiring higher education to produce more information for potential learners. These include:

- Teaching Quality Assessment ratings for each department. The method for securing these is changing, but it is always worth asking about the latest information.

- What do the courses offered by your department include in their 'Programme Specifications'? This should give you a clearer idea of what and how you will learn.

- From 2002, all students in HE will have a Transcript of Attainment, which will give greater detail than a simple degree classification on what you have actually learned. What is or isn't included in the transcript for your university or department?

- From 2005, all students in higher education will have the chance to record and reflect on their learning through materials and processes which encourage 'Personal Development Planning'. This is central to your employability, since it helps you to identify, articulate and evidence the knowledge, skills and experience you gain while studying. What plans does your university or department have for introducing these processes?

Some of this information is not particularly easy to obtain at the present time – which, for those of you interested in your employability, makes it all the more important to ask for!

Do not – NOT – apply for a vocational course unless you are absolutely certain that you want to do that job (based on the research described above) and that it is likely to exist in a familiar form by the time you graduate.

In the UK, unlike mainland Europe, we have a substantially 'any discipline' graduate job market. Over 40 per cent of all graduate vacancies advertised through the main channels are open to graduates of any discipline. If you add to this the wide range of postgraduate vocational courses, from Law to Librarianship, Journalism to Social Work, that you can enter with any degree subject, the actual range of opportunities in the UK available to graduates of all disciplines will be round about 70 per cent of the total occupational opportunities.

This means that, unless you have made an informed decision to enter one of the comparatively few professions that *require* a particular first degree (most of the medical, land use and engineering fields) you will have far greater flexibility with a degree which will open many doors and which you have studied for love of the subject.

Employability is high on the Government's agenda for higher education and many new initiatives are in development even as you read these pages. The next edition of this book will inevitably describe far more formal and integrated opportunities within the academic curriculum to become aware of what you are gaining from your degree.

. . . Academics

'What is the research methodology?' I am sure you will be asking – especially if your university or college does not feature highly in the statistical tables for your subject. For answers to such questions, look at pages 24 and 25, which outline the key factors. You can also visit www.careers-portal.co.uk/earning or write to Cliff Pettifor at Trotman.

This apart, there are a number of key messages for academics in these pages:

First of all, the very existence of this book reminds us that employability is becoming an important criterion for selecting institution or subject – If you really care about your discipline, *what are you, your LISN Subject Centre and your department doing to make it easy to see what someone taking your course can gain from the experience?*

The heart of employability lies in good learning – and in the student being aware of what they are gaining in knowledge, skills and experience. How easy is it for them to make sense of your subject's Benchmarking statements? Your course Programme Specification? A Philosophy course is an excellent basis for developing higher-level skills including communication and problem solving, but how would a potential applicant know this?

The employability agenda does not, I believe, require that traditional disciplines and learning approaches are tossed aside – rather, that they need to be explained in ways that make sense to a new generation of learners.

Partnerships with employers that are more sophisticated and challenging than a few talks on the skills employers require are also worth exploring. One Geography degree has replaced its Urban Hydrology module with a long case study which delivers all the learning outcomes in the Programme Specifications through a real-world scenario with data supplied by a company.

Do you know what your graduates have gone on to do? Increasingly, academics are developing interest in alumni surveys – but it is still possible for an experienced Law lecturer to believe that 100 per cent of his or her students went into legal professions, when the reality was closer to 40 per cent!

. . . Employers

Yes, it costs a lot of money to recruit a graduate – up to £15,000 for the selection process alone. Taking into account the complexity of the factors outlined in this book that help develop graduates who are able to contribute to your company, are you sure that you are not missing a few tricks?

Of course, it costs money to find out what changes are taking place in university teaching practices, and resources to make real, effective contributions to the academic curriculum . . . but if this book has a message for employers, it is that there is no single, simple – or cheap – way to identify the employable graduate. The challenge inherent in pages 18–21 (*'Despite Government pressure to the contrary, the last five years has seen universities do only very little in the way of formally addressing the development of employable skills'*) is not to higher education alone. It is through partnerships with higher education, based on an understanding of the academic process, that many successful graduate recruiters are influencing the higher education experiences of future graduates.

. . . And finally

Anyone entering higher education for the first time now will find that this is far from their last decision about where and what to learn. For anyone who aspires to employability, *Life Long Learning* is a reality. The pace of technical, economic and social change is now such that many of us will be working in jobs in the future which do not yet exist, using skills that it is impossible to imagine today.

Even now, this is happening – who knew, fifteen years ago, what it was to work in a Call Centre or be a Financial Adviser? Yet now these are among the fastest growing occupations. Even those who have remained in the 'same job' – e.g. teaching, banking, retailing – will know how profound the changes in their working lives have been.

Adding to skills and knowledge for the work place is now an ongoing process. Choosing the right route for individual career development will require all the skills, all the sorts of information, offered in this book. This is the first step.

Val Butcher
Senior Adviser for Employability with the Generic Centre of the UK LTSN (Learning and Teaching Support Network), and a consultant to higher education in matters relating to employability in the academic curriculum.

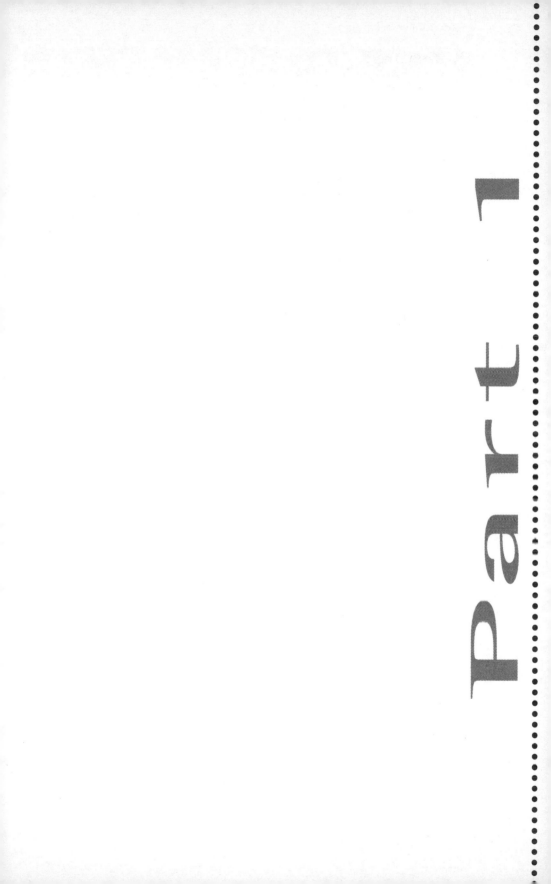

Part 1

1. Introduction to Part 1

Graduate *n* 1 a person who holds a university or college degree.
– Collins Concise English Dictionary

Traditional thinking would have it that there is an aura around the word *'graduate'*. A powerful term, 'graduate' represents a certain calibre or quality for anyone lucky enough to have it bestowed upon them and it brings with it certain expectations as to their future prospects. In these terms, to be a graduate is of no small consequence – even Hollywood saw fit to name a film after it!

Such a perception probably dates from days gone by when graduates were an exclusive bunch – an elite few selected from the upper levels of society to spend some time broadening their minds and experience in preparation for becoming intellectual, spiritual and cultural leaders. Of course, this is no longer the case. Higher education and the status of 'graduate' are no longer preserves of the elite (at least, not usually) and there are now more students watching the daytime schedules than ever before.

The present government intends to get 50 per cent of young people into university by the year 2010. Whether or not this target will be met remains to be seen, but it can't be denied that the last ten years or so have witnessed an explosion in student enrolments: there are now more than 1.2 million people in full-time higher education (and a further 790,000 studying part-time). But what do all these people expect to get out of their degree? What does being a 'graduate' mean to them? *Why do they go to university*? Is it:

- to continue studying a subject that interests them?

- to have a lesson in life, away from the comforts of home?

- to stimulate and develop their general intellect?

- to train for a specific job?

- because it's expected, or a natural progression?

- to delay 'working' for a living?

- to make new friends?

- for the social life?

- to improve general job prospects?

While all these responses can be true – and indeed most of them come into play for *all* prospective students – it is commonly held that the main reason the nation's youth put themselves through the indignity of mounting debt and wearing a silly gown is to improve their chances of long and rewarding careers on the other side. And while perhaps being a 'graduate' isn't quite the same as it once was, it still makes a difference.

Graduates have always occupied a position in the labour market quite apart from the rest of the workforce. Job advertisements regularly ask for a first degree as a matter of course and terms such as 'graduate job' and 'graduate salary' are rife. Indeed, graduates aged 25–29 years earn 29 per cent more than comparable school-leavers, and in general can expect to earn 35 per cent more than the national average. And of course graduate recruitment is a significant part of many a company's human resources activities.

Lying behind this phenomenon are the reasons why graduates are 'special'. They bring with them to a job qualities, skills and experience usually lacking in school leavers and other non-graduates. Like a fine wine, they have spent three or four of their most formative years maturing; learning; improving. They have had the opportunity to stretch themselves, as well as become at least partial experts in their chosen fields.

Graduates' broader range of knowledge and experience stands them in good stead when it comes to adapting to the unfamiliarity of a professional working environment. The research, analytical and communication skills developed as part of a higher education qualification are a crucial part of learning the ropes quickly and becoming a valuable addition to the employer's business.

And until recently, the graduate's unique position has been a charmed one. Employers have maintained the high regard for graduates that dates back to those heady days of 'the elite'. They have readily provided graduates with the penultimate step in the production line of BIRTH > SCHOOL > UNIVERSITY > CAREER > DEATH!!!

Until recently, that is.

The last ten or twenty years have seen a number of significant developments in the worlds of work and higher education. Practices, perceptions and policies have all shifted, this way and that, resulting in a two-pronged attack on the graduate labour market. And the case of the privileged graduate simply walking into gainful employment has effectively gone the way of the dodo.

1. Changes in employment practices

Dramatic developments in technology, the advent of the global economy, the rise of the consumer, the growth in outsourcing and contract/consultative work ... The nature of businesses and employment has changed beyond recognition compared with previous generations. The 'job for life' is no more, and the production line consists of more than the five simple stages. Job security in the traditional sense is largely a thing of the past as employers chase the Holy Grail of 'cost effectiveness' and employees take responsibility for their own career development and progression, learning how to market themselves and remain employable.

The graduate job market has not managed to escape these developments. Far from it in fact – rather than annually harvesting the latest crop of graduates, recruiters are now taking more care over their application and selection procedures, spending vast sums of money to ensure that they attract only the cream of the talent. The upshot is that new generations of

graduates must be more wary of their positions and devote previously unnecessary thought to what their qualifications mean, and what they do after collecting their certificates.

2. Growth in higher education

Participation in higher education has grown spectacularly since the latter half of the 1980s. The replacement of the O-level with the GCSE ratcheted up the proportion of students staying on to take A-levels, which in turn fed universities and colleges with a huge number of fresh faced undergraduates. The six years immediately following the GCSE reforms of 1988 saw an incredible 67 per cent increase in the number of students, and while the rate of change has slowed considerably in the ensuing years, uptake is once again starting to grow at an increasing rate – 5.5 per cent more students will be starting a course in 2002 than at the same time last year.

This is all part of a set of expansionist policies, administered by successive governments, culminating in the target of getting 50 per cent of young people in university or college by the end of this decade. There is little doubt that this is a noble crusade – an educated society can only mean good things for the culture and economy – but it has also served to move the goalposts for the humble graduate. There are now many thousands more graduates competing for the pick of the jobs and they are rapidly coming to realise that their graduate status is no longer the indicator of intellectual superiority it once was. As a result, employers are using other ways of identifying the cream of the crop.

Combining these two factors results in a situation whereby new and future graduates must adapt to the conditions, altering their behaviour to ensure that their qualifications continue to imbue them with something special. It is becoming increasingly apparent to both the students themselves and the institutions that teach them that it is no longer enough to be merely a graduate. To take a place among the elite few who manage to snap up the most coveted jobs, and even to succeed in a more mainstream graduate position, the time spent at university or college must provide whatever is necessary to be a *successful* graduate; an *employable* graduate.

It is these issues that the remainder of this book will explore. How do you become an employable graduate? How can you set yourself on the road to that long and rewarding career?

First and foremost we need to explore what it means to be employable – such an important concept in today's forever-shifting labour market. Only by knowing something of what is required of you will you be able to work towards achieving it. Then we will address ways of reaching that goal, both through your choice of course (subject *and* university) and how you conduct yourself once there – what kind of research you need to do, what extra-curricular activities you can get involved in, how these relate to your employability, the benefits of work experience, and so on.

In Part 2 we take these issues a step further and survey the perceptions of graduates and more than 200 graduate recruiters. Their responses indicate which qualities they value most in new recruits and, in their opinion, which institutions produce the most employable graduates in a number of different subject areas – information that can guide you in your research of suitable courses and perhaps point you in the direction of employability heaven!!!

WARNING: Before reading on, remember this: you should always bear in mind that the ultimate responsibility for your development into a well-rounded and employable graduate lies with *you*. A university, or course, or department, or tutor can provide you with the necessary environment and basic tools, but it is *you* who must use them to your advantage.

2. What Makes a Graduate Employable?

'To be employed is to be at risk, to be employable is to be secure.'
– Director, US Employer Association

All jobs require the employee to have certain skills and attributes that enable them to do their work properly. A chef, for instance, needs to know how to wield a kitchen knife, a footballer should know how to kick a ball without falling over, and an accountant needs to be able to, well, account for things. These are specific skills, unique to their own particular jobs, but there are also many skills and personal qualities that are common to most, if not *all*, jobs.

Graduate jobs in particular are conspicuous in their use of such qualities. To be *truly* employable, the graduates that fill these jobs should be capable of doing not only their own job but at least a hundred others besides. As Carl Gilleard, the Chief Executive of the Association of Graduate Recruiters, points out in his Preface to this book, they must possess a portfolio of skills such that they are flexible enough to adapt to any number of positions and situations. In having these qualities employable graduates bring real value to any job, and make themselves much sought-after commodities in the labour market. And so we have the basis for a successful career.

So, what are these precious skills and where can we get some? They must be truly rare if they really bring such good fortune to anyone lucky enough to possess them. Well, not necessarily. The *transferable* skills (so called because they are transferable between jobs) that define general employability are more often than not the simple things that everyone can do if they put their minds to it – elements of common sense put into the context of the workplace.

VERBAL COMMUNICATION

One of the most important qualities you can have, not just at work but in life, is the ability to communicate clearly. Often taken for granted, mastering communication skills is vital if you are to become an employable graduate. The way you interact with other people (colleagues, customers, suppliers etc.) makes a huge difference to how successful you are at your job. You can find out what other people need from you. You can tell them what it is that *you* want. You can let others know about the ideas you have. You can be confident that your colleagues and clients are *happy* to deal with you. And all with the minimum of fuss – no wasted time for the good communicator.

Talking

The way you speak can heavily influence whether people want to spend time working with you. This is nothing to do with accents, nor is it only about not mumbling. You need to be able to communicate your thoughts in such a way as to allow people to understand what it is you're trying to say. It may sound simple, but it is amazing how many people don't get it right.

When you are talking to someone, always consider the fundamentals of effective communication:

- **Clarity:** People need to hear the words you're saying!

- **Sincerity and honesty:** No one likes to be misled or, worse, lied to.

- **Acceptable vocabulary:** Don't use words likely to offend or confuse.

- **Enthusiasm:** If *you* don't care about what you're saying, no one else will.

- **Humour:** Makes people more willing to listen and stops boredom creeping in.

If you stick to these basic rules then your colleagues and clients will not only understand what you're saying, they will actually *want* to listen to you. Such an environment allows both parties to do their job effectively. Of course, once you get to know people, it may be that you develop a particular style of talking to them but that doesn't mean that you can lose sight of the basics – they still have to be able to understand you or you're both wasting your time.

Listening

Silly as it sounds, communication is a *two-way* process. It requires that someone talks while someone else listens. But listening doesn't just mean keeping your mouth shut while you're being spoken to, it's a little more involved than that. To be a good listener you must take in every word that is said and *make sure* that you understand what you're being told. If necessary, ask for clarification, or make notes to help you remember. When it is time for you to respond, you should do so clearly, sticking to the issues raised.

Body language

This is the most difficult element of good communication to master, but perhaps the most important. When you have a conversation, it is actually your body that does much of the talking, subconsciously sending messages to your companion. Actually controlling your body language is near impossible but there are a few things you can try to avoid:

- Never put your hand over your mouth while you're talking – not only does it make it difficult to hear what you are saying but it also gives the impression that you are not being truthful.

- Don't cross your arms or legs – it is an aggressive way of defending yourself against your subject, making them feel unwelcome in the conversation.

- Try not to let your eyes wander when you are talking or listening – it's very distracting and indicates that you would rather be elsewhere. Focus your attention on the person you're talking to – but don't stare!

- If you touch the top of your head it means you're nervous – this won't necessarily instil confidence in your fellow conversationalists.

WRITTEN COMMUNICATION

Written communication may not be something that you have had too much experience with before joining the workforce – certainly not as much experience as you will have had communicating verbally! But it is an extremely significant part of nearly every graduate job, whether in an office, a laboratory or a chemical plant. The kinds of things that call for good written communication skills include:

- business letters

- faxes

- memos

- emails

- reports

- proposals

- presentations.

The fundamentals of verbal communication also apply here but with a few additional considerations. Different forms of written communication require different approaches. Business letters, for example, should usually be written in a fairly formal style, while emails tend to be shorter and more colloquial. You also need to pay close attention to presentation – e.g. type of paper, handwriting, structure, headings, spelling, grammar etc. You can find more advice about how to communicate in this way – structuring business letters and presentations in particular – in some of the further resources listed towards the back of this book.

ORGANISATION/TIME MANAGEMENT

You could have all the communication, problem-solving and team skills in the world but if you can't organise yourself and find the time to actually use them then they're no use to anyone. By giving you the space in which to showcase your other skills, the ability to organise yourself and manage your time is an invaluable addition to your armoury. Being well organised means that you can find relevant information quickly and on request. Good time management allows you to complete and deliver work on time – there should not be any reason why you can't make good on your promises.

Much like the ability to communicate, good organisational and time management skills work by instilling confidence in others. If you are able efficiently and effectively to execute your tasks then your colleagues, customers, clients, whoever, will trust you to deliver the goods and be happy to work with you.

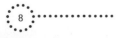

TEAMWORKING

A recent development in the workplace has been the advent of the 'team' ethic, as opposed to the traditional hierarchical structure. The sense now is one of a single team working towards a set of common goals rather than a group of employees working to implement the plans of an anonymous board of directors. To have good team skills is thus to be able to operate in a modern working environment.

Teamwork is not just about getting on well with those around you – although this is very important – it is about being part of a well-oiled machine, and complementing the other parts, which can come in all shapes and sizes. You not only need to know your own role and how it relates to the team, you also need to be aware of where everyone else fits in so that you can allow/help them to do their part effectively. You have to be flexible and resilient enough to go along with the team consensus, even if you are in disagreement. And you will find that effective communication comes in handy in a team situation, not least because conflict avoidance and resolution are often required.

PROBLEM SOLVING

In some jobs, such as those in the IT and engineering industries, solving problems is what it's all about. But it is certainly not a practice restricted to these areas, and the ability to spot and work around or through problems is very useful in more typical working environments.

Imagine you have just started your dream job but are hit by a snag in the first week. Your supplier might have doubled its quote, or a client may not be happy with the standard of work your company is providing, or you have been asked how to improve profitability without additional resources . . . Whatever it is, if you are unable to find a solution or a compromise then you will be stuck. You won't be able to sweep it under the carpet – there *has* to be some kind of resolution. If you have the requisite skills then that resolution needn't result in you and your employer losing out.

IT/COMPUTING

Information and communications technologies are now such an integral part of the contemporary workplace that it is hard to think of a time when computers were new. Similarly, the ability to use such technologies is often taken for granted. But the importance of such skills should never be ignored. From making a telephone call to programming a website, if you weren't capable of using the technology necessary for your job – or at least in a position to learn – you wouldn't get very far in your career. This is what 'computer literacy' means, using technology as a basic tool to do your work, like reading and writing.

And while technology continues to develop at a frightening pace you need to be able to take on board any new developments and learn to use them *effectively* without delay. For example, using the Internet in a professional capacity isn't just about surfing a selection of

Hungarian websites for a couple of hours; it is about finding the information you need for your work quickly and efficiently.

CONFIDENCE

Confidence is different from other skills and qualities. In fact it is probably the foundation of *all* skills. It is difficult to be a good communicator if you are afraid to make your point. It's not easy being a team player when you don't believe you deserve to be a member. Problems get harder to solve if you're not sure you can handle them. Changing jobs is very daunting if you don't think you're up to the challenge. And so on . . .

If you are confident – and confidence comes with experience – then not only will you be better at your job but you will also enjoy it more. This reflects itself in your enthusiasm and motivation, both of which are prevalent qualities in an employable graduate.

BUSINESS AWARENESS

Whether in finance, retail, advertising, engineering, science, the media or law, so many graduate jobs are built on exactly the same principle: business. If you are not aware of the reasons behind your employer's existence, or where they fit into the bigger commercial picture then you are not going to be as effective an employee as you could be.

If a potential recruiter is to find you employable they need to be confident that you will come into their organisation with a working knowledge of how businesses operate. You need to be aware of what their aims are, how these aims are achieved, who their customers are, the importance of budgets, and so on and so forth.

LANGUAGES

Apart from specialist areas like translating, interpreting and linguistics, the need for language skills is not usually absolute. However, as the world gets smaller and more and more companies find themselves dealing in overseas markets, the value of having a multilingual workforce is increasingly significant. If you can offer an employer a second language as an additional string to your bow, they will only think the better of you for it.

SELF-AWARENESS

Being aware of who you are and what you're capable, and incapable, of is the first step in having a successful and rewarding career. An exploration of all the elements of self-awareness and how they relate to your employability could probably fill an entire book but, for now, it will suffice to say that only through identifying your strengths, weaknesses, ambitions and responsibilities can you begin to develop and use the skills and qualities mentioned here. And going to university or college is perhaps the single best way of 'finding' yourself in existence . . .

DON'T JUST TAKE OUR WORD FOR IT . . .

Dr Andrew Bottomley is Head of Graduate Recruitment Marketing at PricewaterhouseCoopers, one of the biggest employers of graduates in the UK. Here's what he had to say on the subject of graduate employability:

'First and foremost, PricewaterhouseCoopers considers graduates of *any* degree discipline and institution – it would be a poorer place if we didn't. We value diversity and are always mindful of the risk that all our people will think in exactly the same way.

What is more important than a graduate's degree is his or her ability to demonstrate the core qualities, or competencies, that we base our operations on:

1. Commercial awareness – applicants should be able to discuss any opportunities they have had to appreciate a commercial environment (this can take any form, even stacking shelves at Tesco). In particular, they should think in terms of what they have learned. In addition, we would expect graduates to keep themselves informed of current commercial issues by reading the quality broadsheets.

2. Commitment to career – to be successful at PwC is to be in it for the long haul. It is a demanding process that calls for no small amount of commitment and enthusiasm. We would take relevant professional qualifications as an indicator of such attributes.

3. Communicate with impact – our graduate recruits find themselves in 'client-facing' situations only a few weeks into their time here. It is important therefore that they are already able to communicate with impact – that is, both confidently and accurately.

4. Flexibility – in their first year at PwC, new employees move around a lot, from project to project and client to client. They need to be capable of thriving in doing so.

5. Integrity and trust – PwC is hired by clients as a trusted professional adviser and it is essential that we are 100 per cent confident of our employees' integrity. This includes considerations of the validity of applicants' qualifications.

6. Intellect – This does not just mean 'qualifications'. While academic achievement is certainly important, and is one of a number of pre-selection criteria, we like to see graduates who *apply* their intellect and are capable of continual and reflective learning.

7. Motivation and initiative – An employable graduate is not one who just sits there waiting to be told what to do. He or she must have the enthusiasm to define their own roles and what they can do for our clients.

8. Teamwork and collaboration – PwC is a totally team environment – i.e. we cannot achieve our objectives if everyone works alone. In fact, both colleagues and clients appraise our employees for interpersonal as well as technical skills.

These are the essential skills and qualities we think an employable graduate should have. Indeed our, and many others', application forms ask that all answers be related to these competencies.'

'It's far more important to understand yourself than your subject while at college.'
– Personnel Manager, Next

Despite having the once-in-a-lifetime opportunity to develop their skills and personality, many students do not make the most of their three or four (or more) years at university or college. They are not helped by the low provision of formal extra-curricular learning opportunities by most institutions, but even then probably less than 10 per cent take advantage of the personal development training programmes available to them. And it has been estimated that in many universities, less than 2 per cent of students receive *any* significant form of structured personal skills development outside their course content.

There are, of course, many other, less formal, activities that contribute towards personal development that students can get involved with, but again only if they can be bothered. If you want to make the most of your time as a student and come out the other side as a fully employable trailblazer of a graduate, then you are most likely going to have to take responsibility for your own development – for the time being at least it is very rare for personal skills development to be a compulsory part of a degree course (although there are moves afoot to rectify this in time for 2005).

So, what can you do? Well, deciding you are going to do *something* is half the battle. There are so many opportunities available to the average student that it is relatively easy to get into something once you are interested. However, it is important to remember that you only get out what you put in; it is not enough just to do something for the sake of it. Think about how important self-awareness is to your employability and career – you need to be aware of what it is you are doing in terms of your learning and personal development. Always be mindful of how your time at university or college relates to your future employability.

The following are a few examples of the types of employability-enhancing activity you can get involved with at university or college. Bear in mind though that while such opportunities are rife whenever there's a gathering of students nearby, their extent and quality will vary according to institution. We will explore how to research individual institutions in the next chapter. In the meantime, if you make the most of your opportunities they will become valuable additions to your CV – not only will they provide you with some of the skills you need, but also with the *firm evidence* of these skills that potential employers require.

WORK EXPERIENCE

It is important not to underestimate the significance of work experience, and while you don't have to be at university to indulge, there is certainly no better time for it.

In a recent survey of graduates*, many commented that it had taken some time before they felt at home in the labour market and ready for the world of work, because they lacked sufficient experience of a working environment. Even simple skills such as being able to use general office equipment were lacking in some graduates who had no experience of an office environment:

'I didn't feel equipped when I left university; I couldn't use a fax or the photocopier when I got my first job. That made me feel silly; there were all these other people in the office . . . thinking "there he is, got a university degree and can't even use a fax".'
– Business Studies graduate, new university

Graduates also commented on the difference between possessing the theoretical know-ledge gleaned from their degree and being able to put it into practice within the workplace. This has a lot to do with the time it takes to develop confidence, something that a work experience placement can help provide bags of.

'I had the ability, and the qualifications, and plenty of potential . . . what I didn't have was experience of the workplace which would have given me the confidence to go out and find a job with much less stress and delay.'
– Geology graduate, old university

However, there are only a relatively small number of courses that feature a substantial period of work experience. Many graduates taking part in the survey indicated that they would have preferred, with hindsight, to do a sandwich course that would have provided them with the appropriate opportunity. This was particularly the case amongst graduates of vocational degrees, who felt that they lacked relevant experience on leaving university or college, despite their strong theoretical knowledge.

'What was missing was some work experience; I missed out on that, and found it hard to get work as a result. A sandwich course would have been easier and more effective for me.'
– Accountancy graduate, new university

Of course, not all degree subjects lend themselves to structured work experience. And we would certainly not advocate that you abandon your preferred subject in favour of something that does not interest you purely to undertake a sandwich course. So, if you find yourself without the chance to take part in a formal work placement scheme, you can always take advantage of the plentiful casual and part-time job opportunities available to students. Indeed, many undergraduates, faced with mounting debts, find themselves with little choice in the matter. It is essential, however, that in doing so you remain switched on and don't just treat such jobs as brainless sources of funding.

'I felt equipped for work . . . I had always worked through university, in pubs and nightclubs in the evenings, and agency work in offices, mostly admin work . . . I could never envisage a career so I got out there and saw what work was, and learned how to do things.'
– Philosophy graduate, old university

---

* DfEE-CSU-AGCAS-IER Moving On – Graduate Careers Three Years after Graduation

No matter how insignificant and menial the task, if you spend time and thought reflecting on it you are sure to find some positive aspects that you can apply to your personal development. For instance, it is relatively easy to look at a day's work, wherever it is, in terms of time management, communication and teamwork.

You could also look into other forms of work experience such as voluntary work, self-employment, working abroad, vacation work, in fact any situation that will allow you to apply your skills and knowledge in a practical setting. In addition to providing you with confidence, it will also be useful in terms of exploring different career options, developing new skills, gaining evidence of your abilities, building a network of contacts and so on.

FORMAL COURSES

Presently, very few undergraduate courses actually include a personal skills development module. The Centre for Recording Achievement is in the process of developing a system for formal provision of Personal Development Planning (PDP) in higher education, but this is a few years off coming into effect yet. In the meantime, spurred on by governmental pressure, an increasing number of universities and colleges are offering special awards or certificates, often developed in conjunction with local businesses and industry. These include the City & Guilds Personal Development Award and Edexcel's BTEC Professional Development Certificate in Work Based Experience.

Alternatively, for the last three years the National Union of Students (NUS) has been running the National Student Learning Programme (NSLP). This is a scheme that brings extra-curricular key skills training to the masses via individual student unions and a network of student trainers. To date more than 900 student trainers located in over 75 universities have trained in excess of 18,000 of their peers in various key skills. This is a young but successful scheme and well worth further investigation – talk to individual student unions or visit www.nusonline.co.uk/nslp for more information.

The drawback to these courses and schemes and others like them is that they require a substantial commitment from participating students. In some cases special skills courses require an additional 500 hours study time over the course of a degree. That is in addition to the time and effort students spend studying for their main degree, socialising, taking part in clubs and societies (see below), holding down part-time jobs and, if they're lucky, sleeping. Faced with such a situation it's not surprising that the take-up for these courses is low and drop-out rates are high. Nevertheless, *at certain universities and colleges* the opportunities are there if you think they will suit you – and after all, in juggling your commitments you will be learning a valuable lesson in time management.

CLUBS AND SOCIETIES

Perhaps the most accessible way of developing your employability at university is to join a student club or society. At most universities there are literally hundreds of organisations you can join – ostensibly to meet like-minded people and have a good time – and almost

without exception they will provide you with ample opportunity to develop and demonstrate your skills for the benefit of future employers.

For example:

- **sports and games** – from football and rugby to chess, there are usually clubs and teams for all levels of ability and competitiveness

- **student union** – represent your kinsmen and experience how committees function, all at the same time

- **debating society** – perfect preparation for future Members of Parliament and invaluable for negotiation and presentation skills

- **magazines and newspapers** – nearly every university and college has some form of student communication just crying out for editorial and sales staff

- **rag** – charitable student organisation that uses raising cash as an excuse to do some very embarrassing things indeed

- **subject societies** – explore and learn more about the areas that appeal to you by joining up with fellow interested parties.

Not only will taking part in such activities be hugely enjoyable, it will put you in a position where you can learn more about yourself, develop a range of new skills and experience, operate as part of a team – perhaps as leader – improve your confidence and, most importantly, provide you with evidence of your development, something that will put you ahead of the crowd with employers.

You will have the chance to develop:

- **technical skills** such as newspaper or film production

- the ability to handle **group/team dynamics**

- **communication skills**

- **planning and organisational skills**

- **time management skills** amounting to more than 'hockey in winter and tennis in summer'!

You can even take it a step further by standing as a senior member such as president, treasurer or secretary. Or perhaps you can start your own society, or at least help to recruit new members to the existing one. The possibilities to impress potential employers are almost endless. And, as long as you are aware of how all your activities potentially relate to your employability, they won't be disappointed.

PROJECTS

Project work is now a feature of many, if not most, university and college courses. For example, many degrees require, or allow, students to research and write a dissertation. Then there are specific project modules or general coursework. Whatever form it takes, project work represents a golden opportunity to develop and show off your talents. For one thing, you don't have the option of not doing it!

To get the most out of your project work, you need to consider:

- **choosing your project wisely** to ensure that it addresses areas you wish to improve on or demonstrate

- **planning and time management** – both should feature heavily

- **bridging the gap** between academic and professional work

- **presentation and communication** – vital in a good quality project.

If you are clever and go about it the right way, you can thus use your time spent on project work to develop your self-reliance, IT skills, organisational skills, team skills, research skills, time management skills, presentation and communication skills, and so on.

COURSE REPRESENTATION

Each course usually has a staff-student liaison committee that selected students can sit on to represent the views and concerns of their peers regarding the way the course is delivered. This is an excellent way of improving a whole range of skills and a really impressive addition to your body of evidence for prospective employers.

After you have expressed an interest in sitting on such a committee you must then get yourself elected to the post by your fellow students. By doing so, you are immediately exposing yourself to the practices of marketing and selling, thus improving your appreciation and command of these in the process.

Once elected you would then have a number of responsibilities. You would need to identify student concerns regarding the teaching of the course and be prepared to present them to the faculty. This you would do through regular departmental discussions, occasions that would provide you with invaluable experience of formal meetings, presentations, negotiation, budgets and any number of other generic business processes.

You would of course also have to report the results of these meetings back to the students, which again would improve your powers of communication immeasurably, as well as boosting your confidence and assertiveness.

And there is more. We really cannot stress enough what an opportunity time spent studying at university or college can be for the employability-minded individual. And you don't even need to be a seriously focused 'high-flier' to make the most of it. Involvement in clubs and societies, for instance, is first and foremost about enjoying yourself and needn't be a chore designed purely to boost your employment prospects. But with a little bit of thought, even after the fact, you can turn such experiences to your advantage.

DON'T JUST TAKE OUR WORD FOR IT . . .

Dr Andrew Bottomley, Head of Graduate Recruitment Marketing at PricewaterhouseCoopers, believes that it is important to approach higher education with the right attitude:

'Students who are planning on attending university or college must think carefully about what is right for them. They shouldn't allow themselves to be propelled into a specific course by anyone else – being employable is not just about syllabuses and qualifications. They need to think about the kinds of employable qualities we look for as they go through the higher education experience because one thing's for sure, a degree doesn't guarantee you a job.'

4. Finding a Degree Course to Help

'It is our view at UCAS that there is a "top" university or college, or possibly even a top department or faculty, for every individual.'
– Tony Higgins, Chief Executive, UCAS.

When choosing a group of university or college courses to apply to, you must start with the assumption that all institutions are equal. That is your blank canvas. If you begin your research into what is probably the most important decision you have had to make in your life thus far with preconceptions of what the 'top' or 'best' universities are, then you run the risk of missing out on your ideal course.

In truth, there is no such thing as the 'best' university. Every university, every college, every faculty, every department, indeed every lecture theatre and tutor group, is run differently. There are different specialisms, different personalities, different methods, different facilities, different environments and so on. Furthermore, no two students are the same – each individual has different interests, strengths, weaknesses, ambitions, preferences etc. So, it is when you start to think of higher education in this way – as a complex mixture of individuals and institutions, each with their own motivations and capabilities – that the concept of a single 'best' university becomes increasingly unacceptable.

With this in mind, the plethora of well-intentioned university league tables and quality assessments that regularly appear in the national and specialist press, based as they are on only a single factor or small number of criteria, are not ideal ways of making a decision that will profoundly affect your future. You should take any information of this type and carefully apply it to your own circumstances in an effort to discover the best course *for you*. Even the rankings that we include in this book, despite being put together with the ambitions and strengths of the *individual* in mind, should not be taken simply at face value*.

When you research your study options you need to take your blank canvas and, with a completely open mind, use all the available information to assess every possible course according to your specific criteria. You might have to trade off a university or college's reputation against its entry requirements, or the course content against location, and so on – any number of considerations can come into play. In this way you will find that you

---

* UCAS, the Universities and Colleges Admissions Service, is currently in the advanced planning stages of a solution to this quandary. Their idea is to host vast amounts of information on each course and institution electronically, including official data on entry qualifications, employability rates, teaching assessments, research assessments, availability of facilities etc., and then make them available via their website. Potential students and parents would then be able to go online, enter their own preferred criteria and generate their own personal league table of universities and colleges, which they could then edit and update as regularly as necessary. At the time of writing, however, this facility looks like it won't put in an appearance for another 18 months – we hope to bring you more in next year's edition. In the meantime, the *Guardian* newspaper's website http://education.guardian.co.uk features a similar service that they call their 'Interactive University Guide'.

soon arrive at a shortlist that you can investigate further with a view to finding your top course.

And so it is that, keeping these issues in mind, we turn to the single criterion that forms the focal point of this book, namely how time spent in higher education impacts on your future employability, and specifically how your choice of university or college affects your prospects.

In Part 2 of *From Learning to Earning* we will show you how your choice of institution *does* make a difference to your subsequent employability. First, however, we will consider the four ways in which your university or college *can* make a difference and what you need to look out for in your research.

REPUTATION

A number of universities are lucky enough to have good reputations, both with graduate recruiters as well as with the public at large. And some are unlucky enough to have *bad* reputations. Which kind you attend can be an extremely important influence on your perceived employability, as recruiters' opinions of your origins can, and do, count for a lot. Indeed, this is the central premise of the research that appears later in this book. At the very least, which university or college you attended could end up swinging a tight employment decision in your favour.

What to look for

You can start by considering our research, presented in Part 2. It ranks universities, by subject area, according to how employable the recruiters perceive their graduates to be. This is a far more up-to-date and reliable way of judging reputations than simply going with the traditional consensus.

Read around the issue. Newspapers regularly fill their column inches by printing the latest batch of league tables and then discussing them ad infinitum. The broadsheets also have their own special education (and in some cases *higher* education) supplements which often have tasty morsels of relevant information. The league tables themselves can also be a rough guide to university reputation – after all, many recruiters will base their opinions on what they read in the papers.

All the research and newspaper print in the world, however, is no substitute for actually talking to people in the know. If you know anyone involved in recruiting graduates – a friend, a relative, a friend's relative – then get in touch and ask them what the current word on the street regarding university reputation is. They may do nothing more than confirm what you already suspected, but it is better to hear from someone directly involved.

Ask around at the relevant universities and colleges as well. Admissions tutors and careers advisers at the institution should be able to tell you what kind of links and relationships they have with graduate recruiters, or whether recruiters tend to target their graduates. These are very good indicators of university reputation.

COURSE CONTENT

Different institutions teach subjects in different ways. Some choose to emphasise the vocational/employability elements of the subject in their course content – for example, they might include a work placement or a special skills module or project. These are just the sorts of things that will positively affect your subsequent employability.

What to look for

Obviously, you need to pay close attention to what is said in university and college prospectuses and on their websites. These sources will usually contain details of course content. You should pay particular attention to any options you will have in the course of your study so as not to miss anything important – e.g. it might not be immediately apparent that you can choose to take, say, a skills module as part of your second year assessment. If there are gaps in the information provided then give the relevant admissions tutor a call for clarification.

While you have them on the line, ask them about their sandwich courses and work placement schemes. Do they have good links with local industry? Will they find you a suitable placement or will you have to go it alone? Does their scheme allow for proper analysis of the experience? If they mention a few companies that they have links with in this respect, ask them if they mind if you give them a call to get their perspective.

EXTRA PROVISION

Despite government pressure, the last five years has seen universities do only very little in the way of formally addressing the development of employability skills in their students. This is down to a number of obstacles:

- lack of funding for careers services to devote to broader student development

- conflict between main academic studies and non-departmentally organised personal development courses

- disregard for special personal development courses as being a non-essential component of the degree experience

- reluctance on the students' part to attend 'add-on' courses that don't 'count'.

As a consequence, there is a significant disparity in how universities and colleges formally provide for personal skills development.

For example, many universities offer the following services to students outside the main curriculum, usually available through the careers service but sometimes through student unions:

- careers seminars

- aptitude profiling

- careers fairs

- practice interviews

- help with CVs.

Some universities, however, go a bit further and provide students with the opportunity to get together with alumni, who act as mentors or advisers. And the best institutions offer the special personal skills awards or certificates discussed in the previous chapter. If you are prepared to commit the time and effort to these extras then it'll be worth your while to choose a university or college where that option will be available to you.

What to look for

You need to keep your eyes open for indications that your potential university or college falls into the latter group of institutions. Ask the admissions tutors and careers advisers what kind of additional services they provide – and what is the uptake like? Is there a network of alumni? Is the National Student Learning Partnership scheme available?

CLUBS AND SOCIETIES

As we saw in the previous chapter, there are many ways in which you can develop your employability at university or college while having bags of fun! The availability and quality of these opportunities does, however, vary according to where you study. The Oxbridge universities, for example, pride themselves on the many hundreds of committed clubs and societies that can potentially provide a valuable network of contacts. On the other hand, they are not particularly keen on students spending too much time away from their studies. Part-time work in particular, while not an extra-curricular activity in the traditional sense, is frowned upon at these institutions.

What to look for

The student unions should be able to provide you with the most help and information in this respect. Many publish 'alternative prospectuses' with details of the non-academic elements of student life. *The Student Book* (see *Further Resources* at the back of this book) will also provide you with another view of each institution. You should try and talk to existing and former students and get an honest view straight from the horse's mouth. It will also be useful to find out what kind of free time you will actually have to devote to extra-curricular activities – probably best to get this from the staff rather than the students if you want a reliable answer!!!

Of course, these considerations may not be so important to some, but if employability is high up on your 'list of things to get out of higher education' then they are just the sorts of things you should be looking into. And you are bound to discover some more during the course of your research. If you're looking for somewhere to start, then why not try Part 2 ...

DON'T JUST TAKE OUR WORD FOR IT . . .

Richard Illingworth, Recruitment Manager for the Audit Commission, thinks that the quality of extra careers provision varies substantially between universities:

'We have noticed that university careers services and the facilities they provide are mixed. Some are hindered by a lack of funding while others are better at securing the extra money that a high quality service needs. The better ones are more proactive in their activities, engaging students and, most importantly, helping them identify how their course – whatever it is – applies to their employability. It is unfortunate that all too many students have to try and figure this out for themselves.

This is particularly important because more and more application forms are tailored to identifying specific skills, meaning that potential recruits must relate their experiences of higher education to certain competencies. Whether it comes from their course, some work experience or extra-curricular activities, graduates should always use something as evidence of skills development on an application.

Generally speaking, I would say that a large number of organisations are looking for the same general competencies in their new recruits. By using the opportunities that their university affords them to develop and demonstrate their general employability, a single graduate can easily secure offers of employment in, say, three widely different areas. It is then up to the recruiter to train their people in the specific skills required in their business.'

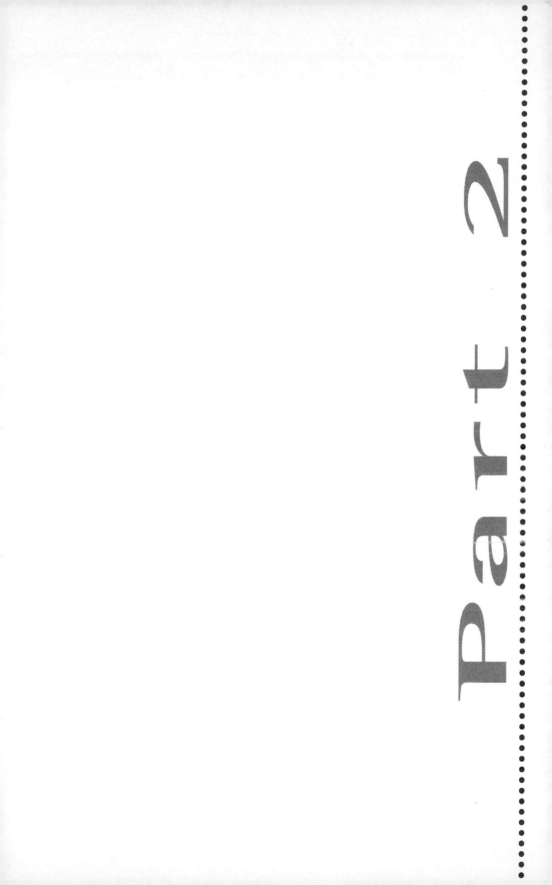

Part 2

5. Introduction to Part 2

In Part 2, we will look at the evidence. We will explore what *really* happens to graduates after they leave university or college to enter the world of work, and how the characteristics of their degrees – subject, result and institution – affect their employability.

THE SHAPE OF GRADUATE EMPLOYMENT

Here we use data which originally appeared in the 1999 publication DfES-CSU-AGCAS-IER *Moving On: Graduate Careers Three Years after Graduation** to establish what the world of graduate employment actually looks like. We examine the extent to which graduates experience unemployment, how much they are paid and the types of jobs they have in the years immediately following their graduation ceremony. What is more, we take a look at the part that degree characteristics have to play in these employment patterns.

The *Moving On* data that we use is particularly reliable in building a picture of graduate employment because, unlike many other reports of graduate destinations and employment available, it accounts for graduates' experiences for up to three years after graduation, and not just the first six months.

Any graduate will tell you that the first six months of working life doesn't always represent the career nirvana. In fact many find themselves unable to decide what to do, or experimenting with careers, or between jobs, or in temporary employment, or taking time out etc., etc. Over time, however, people find their niches – the jobs that suit them. By focusing on the *three years* following graduation, and not just the first six months, we are waiting for the dust to settle and, as a result, get a more realistic impression of how degree characteristics affect subsequent employability.

RECRUITERS' THOUGHTS ON GRADUATE EMPLOYABILITY/WHICH UNIVERSITIES?

For the last 12 years we have been conducting an annual survey of graduate recruiters' perceptions of employability and higher education, and using the results to, among other things, rank universities according to how employable their graduates are. In *Recruiters' thoughts on graduate employability* and *Which universities produce the most employable graduates?*, we present our latest findings, based on the opinions of more than 200 graduate recruiters from throughout the UK over the last three years. (A list of some of the participating recruiters can be found as Appendix C.)

---

*This data is reproduced with the kind permission of original publishers the Department for Education and Skills (formerly Department for Education and Employment), the Higher Education Careers Services Unit, the Association of Graduate Careers Advisory Services and the Institute for Employment Research.

We have asked these recruiters to indicate what they consider enhances a graduate's employability – which skills, qualities and attributes appeal to them. We have asked them whether a graduate's university influences their assessment of that graduate's employability. We have asked them what they think about degree standards and graduates in general. We have asked them whether they think there are certain universities that produce graduates of above or below average employability in a range of subject areas, and whether there are any that they particularly target or avoid. In short we have asked all the questions that you would ask, the difference being that the recruiters have answered, and it is those answers that we present to you here.

In *Recruiters' thoughts* ... we establish a context for the bulk of our results by examining recruiters' opinions of higher education and graduate employability in general. This is followed by *Which universities* ... an extensive collection of tables and charts that explore, subject by subject, which universities the recruiters consider produce the most employable graduates. These subject tables are designed to help you focus your thoughts and research into which path is the one that will take you to the top ...

WARNING: Before reading on, remember this: you should always bear in mind that the ultimate responsibility for your development into a well-rounded and employable graduate lies with *you*. A university, or course, or department, or tutor can provide you with the necessary environment and basic tools, but it is *you* who must use them to your advantage.

6. The Shape of Graduate Employment

So far we have been working under the implicit assumption that a major driver behind individuals choosing to go to university is the promise of improved job prospects upon graduation. Furthermore, we have suggested that choice of course makes a difference to graduates' subsequent employability. But have we been entitled to do so? Think back to page 2. Each one of those reasons for going to university will be the dominant factor for some students. And does it really matter where and what you study or is a degree a degree, no questions?

By examining the fortunes of a group of graduates over a number of years, the research that follows shows us that the characteristics of your degree, such as subject and university, really *do* make a difference to your future employability. And, to start with, Figure 6.1 reveals that a concern for future job prospects is indeed a factor in students' study choices.

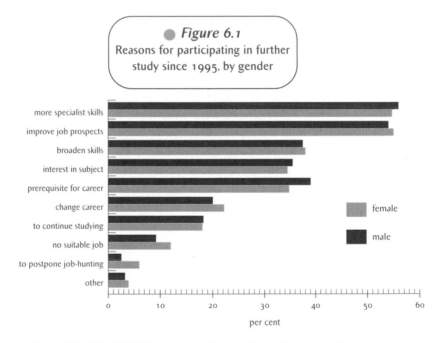

● *Figure 6.1*
Reasons for participating in further study since 1995, by gender

Source: DfEE-CSU-AGCAS-IER Moving On – Graduate Careers Three Years after Graduation 1999

Figure 6.1 illustrates that among those students undertaking further study since 1995 the most popular reasons for doing so were career-related. Over half chose this route in order to acquire more specialist skills and to improve their general job prospects (both 54 per cent). More than a third (36 per cent) took on further study because it was a requirement for their chosen career (e.g. teaching, medicine), while the same proportion thought they should broaden the range of skills they could offer before seeking employment. And while having an interest in the subject motivated 34 per cent of students, 'negative' reasons for participating in further study (no suitable job available, 10 per cent; to postpone job hunting, 4 per cent) appeared well down the list of options.

Figure 6.1 covers students of *all* ages. Closer inspection of the data reveals that wanting to improve job prospects and acquire more specialist skills were key motivations for engaging in further study across all age groups. However, graduates aged 29 and under were more likely to have been interested in improving their job prospects (55 per cent) compared with their mature counterparts. Younger graduates (aged 25 and under) were also significantly more likely to have entered into further study as a prerequisite to entering their chosen career (41 per cent compared with 23 per cent of 40–49 year olds and only 16 per cent of those aged 50+).

It would seem therefore that students are increasingly making their study choices according to how they affect future employability.

Our second assertion – that they are wise to do so – is also borne out by the evidence. In so far as we can use a graduate's employment profile (i.e. any periods of unemployment, type of job and earnings) as indicators of how employable they are, we can investigate the effects of degree characteristics on their employability.

UNEMPLOYMENT

Figures 6.2, 6.3 and 6.4 consider the relationships between the rate at which graduates are absorbed into the labour market and the characteristics of their degrees. By tracking the unemployment experienced by those who graduated in July 1995 over time, we can see how long it takes for them to find employment.

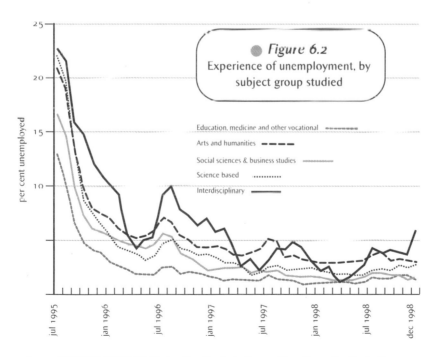

● **Figure 6.2**
Experience of unemployment, by subject group studied

Education, medicine and other vocational
Arts and humanities
Social sciences & business studies
Science based
Interdisciplinary

Source: DfEE-CSU-AGCAS-IER Moving On – Graduate Careers Three Years after Graduation 1999

Figure 6.2 shows the profiles of graduate unemployment broken down by degree subject area. It is clear that those who studied courses specifically preparing them for a career (education, medicine, law etc.) are able to secure work quickly. On the other hand, graduates of arts and humanities and interdisciplinary courses appear to have more difficulties in finding employment. Further data not shown here also tells us that graduates of these subjects are much more likely to spend six months or more in unemployment during the three and a half years after qualifying. However, in Figure 6.2, while subject area certainly seems to make a difference immediately following graduation, that difference is much less significant two years later.

Remember, though, that not being unemployed is not the same as having the job you want. As we shall see later, many graduates sacrifice getting a 'good' graduate job in order to avoid unemployment.

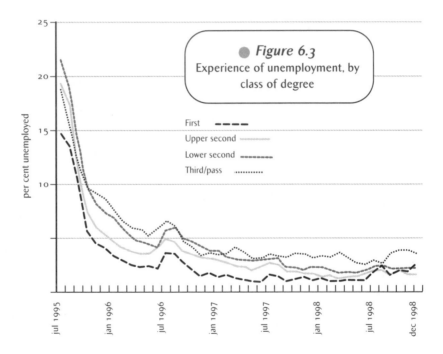

● *Figure 6.3*
Experience of unemployment, by class of degree

First
Upper second
Lower second
Third/pass

Source: DfEE-CSU-AGCAS-IER Moving On – Graduate Careers Three Years after Graduation 1999

Figure 6.3 focuses on how the result of a graduate's degree affects their absorption into the labour market. Generally speaking, the better the degree class, the lesser the experience of unemployment. This is to be expected – a good degree result demonstrates the acquisition of valuable skills and has long been regarded by employers as hard evidence of a potential employee's intelligence and their ability to apply themselves. Similarly, graduates with lower second or third class honours degrees are more likely to be unemployed for six months or more in the three and a half years after qualifying than their higher-achieving counterparts.

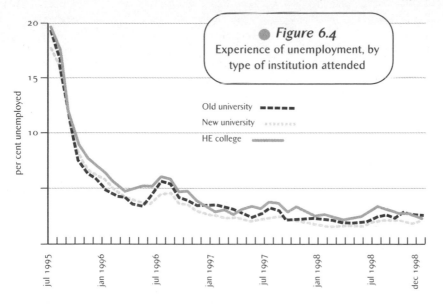

Source: DfEE-CSU-AGCAS-IER Moving On – Graduate Careers Three Years after Graduation 1999

Figure 6.4 lets us see that, contrary to popular belief, graduates of new universities experience no more unemployment than those from the old. The unemployment profiles for each type of higher education institution are almost identical.

However, for our purposes, and as mentioned previously, experiences of unemployment tell only part of the story of graduate employability . . .

TYPE OF JOB

Consider a new graduate who is finding it difficult to get a job in their chosen career, or even a comparable position in another area. Faced with such a dilemma this individual will be likely to accept a 'lesser' job, simply to be able to pay the bills. By their own standards, and by those that we have set, this graduate is not as employable as they would like, despite actually being employed.

A more informative measure of employability would therefore be one based on the *types* of jobs that graduates have attained. Of course, we cannot categorically say what a 'high quality' or 'graduate' job is but we can form an approximation by defining some basic parameters. The survey data in figures 6.5, 6.9 and 6.10 below is based on three such parameters:

1. classifying occupations as:

- *traditional graduate jobs* (those that typically require five years of additional education after the age of compulsory schooling)

- *graduate track jobs* (typically requiring three years of additional education)

- *non-graduate jobs* (typically requiring one and a half years of additional education)

2. graduates' own assessment of whether their job requires a degree level qualification, using skills and subject knowledge acquired during their course

3. earnings at the time of the survey.

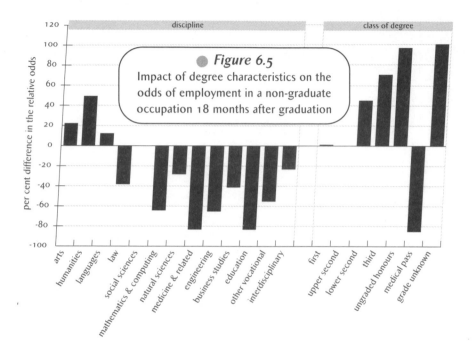

Figure 6.5
Impact of degree characteristics on the odds of employment in a non-graduate occupation 18 months after graduation

NOTE Controlling for other influences (e.g. social background, A-level results) each variable's impact is expressed relative to a reference category, in this case 'social sciences' and 'upper second'. For example, graduates of a humanities course are approximately 50 per cent more likely than social science graduates to have a non-graduate job 18 months after graduation. Similarly, education graduates are about 85 per cent less likely. In this way we can make an effective comparison across characteristics.

Source: DfEE-CSU-AGCAS-IER Moving On – Graduate Careers Three Years after Graduation 1999

Figure 6.5 illustrates the impact of degree subject studied and class of degree achieved on the probability of employment in a 'non-graduate' occupation 18 months after graduation. What it makes clear is that degree subject and result have quite an effect on a graduate's chances in the labour market. Notably, arts and humanities graduates have higher odds of being employed in *non*-graduate occupations, as have those with poorer final degree results.

Figure 6.6 breaks down 'type' of job still further and looks at graduates three and a half years after qualifying. In this case, 'management and administration', 'professional' and 'associate professional' can be classed as graduate jobs; while 'clerical and secretarial' and 'manual, routine service and operative' represent their non-graduate counterparts.

As indicated previously in figure 6.5, a further 18 months on and the arts and humanities areas still have higher proportions of graduates in non-graduate jobs. In light of these results, we can surmise that courses in these areas are less successful in providing graduates with the employability skills and qualities valued by recruiters, whereas business studies graduates appear to be highly valued.

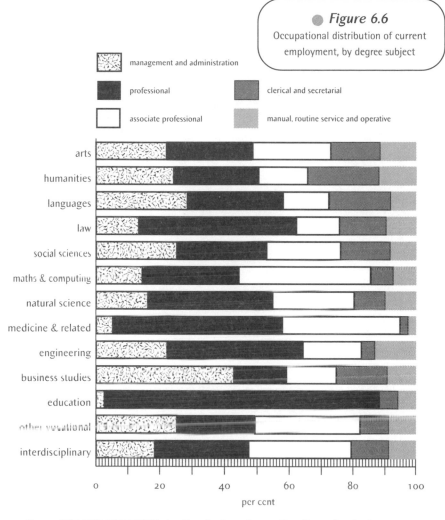

● *Figure 6.6*
Occupational distribution of current employment, by degree subject

management and administration

professional

clerical and secretarial

associate professional

manual, routine service and operative

Source: DfEE-CSU-AGCAS-IER Moving On – Graduate Careers Three Years after Graduation 1999

EARNINGS

The final indicator of graduate employability that we will consider is earnings. Many people consider salary as *the* defining characteristic of a job and/or career – a higher-paying job is better than a lower-paying one and a well-paid graduate must be more employable than one who is comparatively poorly paid. While such a view is in no way an exact representation of the world of work, salary *can* be a useful guide to the status of a job and hence the quality/employability of the employee.

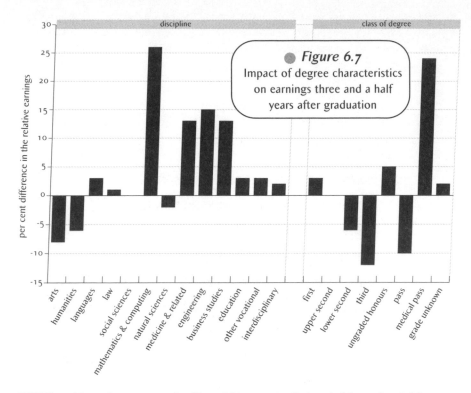

Figure 6.7
Impact of degree characteristics on earnings three and a half years after graduation

NOTE Figure 6.7 uses the same approach as Figure 6.5 in expressing the impact of degree characteristics on earnings relative to two reference categories – 'social sciences' and 'upper second'

Source: DfEE-CSU-AGCAS-IER Moving On – Graduate Careers Three Years after Graduation 1999

Figure 6.7 suggests that graduates in mathematics and computing in particular, but also engineering, business studies and medicine and related subjects, earn a significantly higher amount than graduates in other disciplines. This is perhaps unsurprising as these are the types of courses we would expect to emphasise skills relevant to the workplace, so preparing their graduates for employment. Arts and humanities graduates tend to be the least well paid.

There is also a strong positive relationship with degree performance, graduates who obtained a first class degree earning on average 3 per cent more than graduates with an upper second (2:1), and graduates with a lower second (2:2) earning on average 6 per cent less.

Figure 6.8 translates these findings into terms of cold, hard cash. Once again we can see that, on average, the more vocationally minded areas produce the best-paid graduates. Over a quarter of maths and computing graduates earned more than £30,000 per annum, but at the other extreme only 3 per cent of arts graduates did so. 23 per cent of arts graduates earned an annual salary of less than £12,000 but only 4 per cent of their maths and computing peers did so. It is also notable – unfair, but notable – that in every subject area, male graduates still earn more than their female equivalents.

Degree result is also significant: 15 per cent of those with first class honours earned more than £30,000. The proportion fell by degree class to 5 per cent of those with third class degrees.

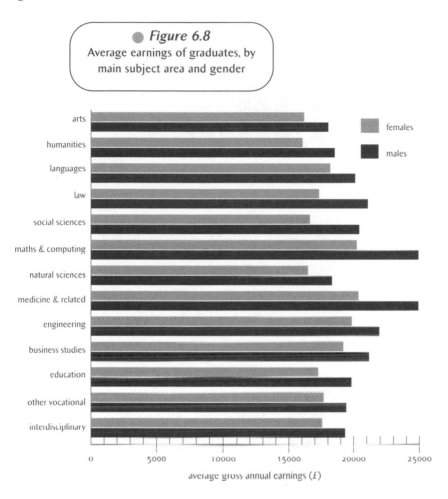

● *Figure 6.8*
Average earnings of graduates, by
main subject area and gender

Source: DfEE-CSU-AGCAS-IER Moving On – Graduate Careers Three Years after Graduation 1999

It is important to remember that financial reward is not the only benefit of graduate employment. Graduates are often motivated by other factors – a happy and employable graduate is not necessarily a particularly well-paid graduate. However, generally speaking, it is clear from the preceding data that the characteristics of your degree, in terms of subject and result, make a difference to your future prospects/employability.

INSTITUTION

But what of that other, all-important, degree characteristic: the awarding institution? In a perfect world the university or college you attend would make absolutely no difference whatsoever to your subsequent employability. In this kind of world a 2:1 in English from Oxford would mean exactly the same as a 2:1 in English from Manchester Met. Of course, in the real word, this is not the case at all.

Rightly or wrongly, there is a hierarchy of universities and colleges, largely based on tradition but also on particular strengths and weaknesses, that moves employers to favour certain institutions and discount others. Regardless of whether or not this is a legitimate practice, the truth is that courses *do* vary a great deal between institutions. Different syllabuses, different teaching staff, different facilities, different levels of student support and so on all mean that the defining characteristic of a degree course tends not to be the subject but the institution. Moreover, there are also countless differences in the non-academic aspects of the time spent in higher education: accommodation, extra-curricular clubs and societies, the social and cultural environment and all the other things that go towards shaping a graduate. Look at it this way and it becomes clear that a 2:1 in English from Oxford is indeed a *very* different beast from a 2:1 in English from Manchester Met.

This doesn't mean that the traditionally highly-regarded institutions are necessarily better in all areas. There are pockets of excellence in some of the less prestigious universities – particularly as far as vocational degree courses are concerned – and weak areas in some of the most elite insititutions. It is thus important to consider universities and colleges in the context of the subject you want to study.

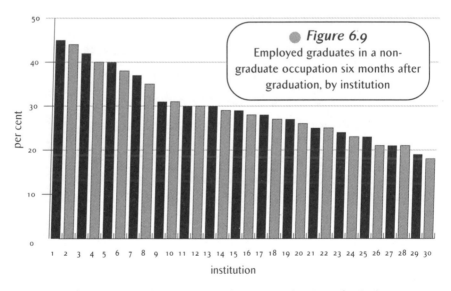

● *Figure 6.9*
Employed graduates in a non-graduate occupation six months after graduation, by institution

Source: DfEE-CSU-AGCAS-IER Moving On – Graduate Careers Three Years after Graduation 1999

Figure 6.9 shows the proportions of graduates in employment in a non-graduate occupation (as defined on pp. 29–30), by institution six months after graduation. The names of the institutions are not included and are instead represented by the numbers 1–30, but this makes no difference to our analysis. What *is* important is that there appears to be a wide variation in non-graduate employment between institutions. The institution with the poorest record had 45 per cent of employed graduates in a non-graduate occupation compared with the institution with the best record of only 18 per cent.

This result confirms that you need to research your choice of university or college thoroughly. You need to find out all you can about how employable each institution can 'make' you. It is particularly useful to learn what kind of reputation each university or college has with employers – and, more importantly, the reputations of individual departments. The research presented in the next chapter is designed to help you in this task.

The data in Figure 6.9, however, does not account for other variables such as graduates' personal characteristics (age, social background, gender etc.) and degree subject. We have already established that degree subject has a significant effect on future employment so it would be wise to remove it and other such variables from the equation when considering the impact of higher education institution alone. Figure 6.10 does just this.

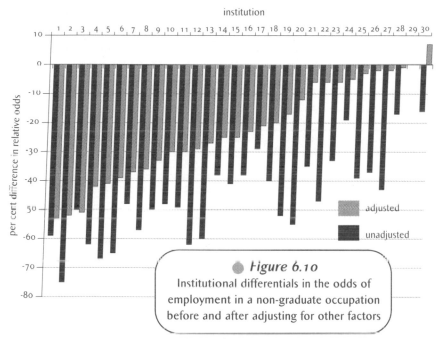

● **Figure 6.10**
Institutional differentials in the odds of employment in a non-graduate occupation before and after adjusting for other factors

NOTE The results in Figure 10 are presented relative to the arbitrarily chosen institution 29. The influence of degree class is not removed on the basis that exam results are part of institution 'output'. However, it could be argued that degree class should be accounted for in its role as an indicator of graduates' innate ability.

Source: DfEE-CSU-AGCAS-IER Moving On – Graduate Careers Three Years after Graduation 1999

The darker columns in Figure 6.10 represent the percentage difference in the probability of being employed in a non-graduate job relative to institution 29 *without* adjusting for other factors (i.e. corresponding to the data in Figure 6.9). The lighter columns represent the same after removing the influence of other variables, like degree subject. In keeping with our previous findings, allowing for these significant variables alters the ordering of the institutions (the numbers 1–30 in Figure 6.9 do not correspond exactly with those in Figure 6.10). However, what is more interesting is that there is *still* a variation. For example, graduates of institution 1 are approximately 53 per cent less likely to be employed in a non-graduate occupation 18 months after graduation than institution 29. On the other hand, graduates of institution 30 are about 6 per cent *more* likely.

This data is not included in order to name and shame specific institutions, but to highlight the fact that the university or college department you attend *does* make a difference in the graduate job market. This might be for historical or traditional reasons, or perhaps some institutions are specialists at producing employable graduates in certain areas, or provide an environment more conducive to imbuing their graduates with employability qualities ... Whatever, the trick is to identify these aspects of a department or institution's character early on in your research and then apply them to your personal circumstances, in terms of your ambition, interests and ability.

MOVING ON

We have seen that if you are intending to use your time at university to enhance your employability, and maximise your prospects in the graduate labour market, you need to pay careful consideration to:

- your choice of subject

- your choice of university or college

- applying yourself effectively once there.

These are the three influential factors over which you have near total control.

To choose a subject is a relatively simple task. Most students will go with something they find interesting and/or is useful/essential for their chosen career, or perhaps something that they already know they are good at. You shouldn't let the data presented in this chapter influence your choice of subject too much. We are not suggesting that you must study business or IT if you want to get a job, but if your preference is for arts and/or humanities subjects, you may have to pay extra attention to developing your employability – if, indeed, this is important to you.

Applying yourself to your studies and personal development at university or college is also relatively easy. It may seem hard sometimes, particularly in the face of happy hour and the lure of a comfortable bed on a cold winter's morning, but a little motivation and discipline go a long way.

Choosing an institution, however, is an altogether more difficult proposition – for most students the universities and colleges of this land are an unknown quantity. Your research should serve to remove this mystery and uncover the elements of institutions that will help you to achieve your aims. We have already touched on the paths this research needs to take in Part 1. One such path is to consider the data presented in the remainder of this book detailing the opinions of graduate recruiters on different universities and degree subjects ...

7. Recruiters' Thoughts on Graduate Employability

Before we explore how recruiters perceive graduates of specific universities it will be useful to find out their general thoughts regarding graduates and employability. Doing this will help to put the subsequent institution-specific data into some sort of context.

EMPLOYER APPEAL

Which skills and features do recruiters feel enhance a graduate's employability?

What a potential employer expects and likes to see in graduates is important to know as it can help you identify your particular strengths and weaknesses, as well as prioritise the areas where there is room for improvement.

TABLE 7.1 EMPLOYABILITY QUALITIES THAT RECRUITERS LOOK FOR IN GRADUATES

Rank	Qualities, skills or attainment sought	% choosing	% 97/98
1	Verbal communication skills	83.8	81.1
2	Enthusiasm	81.5	n/s
3	Written communication skills	71.8	69.5
4	Work experience	69.9	76.4
5	Degree classification	67.6	71.3
6	Problem solving	66.9	n/s
7=	Personal/transferable skills	66.7	66.7
7=	Teamworking	66.7	63.0
9	Numeracy	64.8	n/s
10	Business awareness	62.5	69.9
11	Computing skills	59.3	66.2
12	Self-reliance	54.2	n/s
13	A-level grades	53.7	62.5
14	Course content	30.4	43.1
15	Sandwich course	31.5	23.1
16	Gap year (paid work)	31.0	25.3
17	Sport & hobbies	27.3	27.4
18	Second language	22.7	31.0
19	Gap year (voluntary/unpaid work)	21.3	14.7
20	GCSE grades	17.1	20.4
21	Gap year (travel)	12.5	15.8

n/s = not surveyed

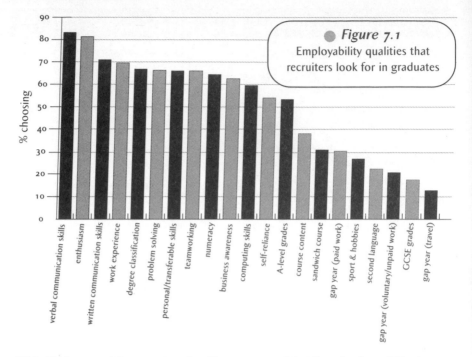

● **Figure 7.1**
Employability qualities that recruiters look for in graduates

While Table 7.1 and the corresponding Figure 7.1 reveal that there has been little change over time in the relative importance of these criteria, there are one or two interesting points to draw out.

It is interesting that both forms of communication feature so highly in the ranking – but not necessarily surprising when you consider that good communication is the skill that effectively binds all the others. After all, what's the use of solving a problem if you can't share the solution? Why bother having a great idea if you are unable to explain it to others? How can you be a team player if no one knows what you're talking about?!

Similarly, enthusiasm is an essential quality to possess if the others are to work. You could have all the skills in the world but if you hate your job and can't be bothered to apply them, then they'll just go to waste. Accordingly, enthusiasm takes its place at number two in our table.

While being vital in the modern workplace, to sell yourself as computer literate no longer helps you to stand out as it once did. Perhaps in recognition of this, fewer recruiters are now picking out computing skills as a desired quality than a few years ago. It is possible that they are now more likely to *assume* that a new graduate would possess the basic skills necessary to operate within the so-called 'paperless office'.

Finally, it seems that recruiters would prefer it if graduates do something more productive than just enjoy themselves during their gap years. Graduates who can show that they have used their year out constructively have a head start over their rivals who spent 12 months sitting in front of the television. And spending a gap year in 'paid work' means more than working part-time behind a bar to fund said TV watching – the work should be challenging and relevant to a graduate career.

However, if you are planning an exciting trip around the world for before or after you attend university or college, you needn't be disturbed by the lowly position of 'gap year (travel)' in our ranking. Time spent travelling is an ideal way of developing many of the other qualities in Table 7.1 – e.g. problem-solving, verbal communication, self-reliance – as well as perhaps identifying what are your weaker areas. As long as you can demonstrate these aspects to a potential employer, taking time out to travel is an excellent way of developing your employability.

SIZE MATTERS

The size of the company they work for makes a big difference to a lot of people. Some feel that they will thrive as a small part of a huge corporate machine, while others prefer to be a big fish in a small pond. It is useful therefore to see how the results in Table 7.1 break down by size of recruiter.

TABLE 7.2 EMPLOYABILITY QUALITIES THAT RECRUITERS LOOK FOR IN GRADUATES, BY RECRUITER SIZE

Quality, skill or attainment sought	All %	Large %	Medium %	Small %
Verbal communication skills	83.8	86.8	86.2	80.0
Enthusiasm	81.5	82.4	82.8	84.0
Written communication skills	71.8	75.0	72.4	69.3
Work experience	69.9	72.1	77.6	62.7
Degree classification	67.6	64.7	79.3	65.3
Problem solving	66.9	72.5	72.7	65.3
Personal/transferable skills	66.7	80.9	69.0	50.7
Teamworking	66.7	73.5	74.1	56.0
Numeracy	64.8	66.2	63.8	68.0
Business awareness	62.5	57.4	72.4	60.0
Computing skills	59.3	58.8	50.0	68.0
Self-reliance	54.2	51.4	60.3	54.7
A-level grades	53.7	58.8	58.6	48.0
Course content	38.4	32.4	39.7	45.3
Sandwich course	31.5	39.7	39.7	18.7
Gap year (paid work)	31.0	33.8	32.8	29.3
Sport & hobbies	27.3	36.8	27.6	17.3
Second language	22.7	27.9	31.0	12.0
Gap year (voluntary/unpaid work)	21.3	26.5	25.9	12.0
GCSE grades	17.1	20.6	17.2	14.7
Gap year (travel)	12.5	20.6	8.6	6.7

NOTE We have arbitrarily defined a large recruiter as one planning on recruiting 21 or more graduates this year; medium 8–20 graduates and small 7 or less. These numbers have been chosen to generate roughly equal samples for each size.

Our idea of what matters will probably differ slightly from yours but we have picked out and highlighted a few interesting points in Table 7.2, including:

- Large companies place a lot of emphasis on *transferable* skills – i.e. those that you can apply to any given situation. This might be because new recruits at bigger organisations tend to be faced with a wider variety of operations.

- Accordingly, large companies are more impressed by gap years spent travelling. As we have already seen, this is an activity that can significantly enhance the ability to adapt to many and varied situations.

- Possibly because of smaller training budgets, small and medium-sized companies are more interested in graduates who come closer to being 'oven-ready' – bringing with them business awareness and computer skills, as well as the experience of a course content more relevant to the work.

REGIONAL DIFFERENCES

It is a matter of opinion as to what extent regional variations in desired employability qualities actually matter. However, if you are confident that you will end up working in a particular area it could be of significant interest.

TABLE 7.3 EMPLOYABILITY QUALITIES THAT RECRUITERS LOOK FOR IN GRADUATES, BY REGION

Quality, skill or attainment sought	All %	North %	Midlands %	South %	London %	Scotland %
Verbal communication skills	83.8	91.3	78.6	84.0	83.3	81.3
Enthusiasm	81.5	91.3	85.7	78.7	73.8	75.0
Written communication skills	71.8	82.6	64.3	72.0	73.8	62.5
Work experience	69.9	60.9	78.6	69.3	76.2	75.0
Degree classification	67.6	65.2	66.7	78.7	59.5	43.8
Problem solving	66.9	54.5	56.7	75.0	63.0	78.6
Personal/transferable skills	66.7	82.6	66.7	61.3	76.2	43.8
Teamworking	66.7	82.6	52.4	69.3	71.4	62.5
Numeracy	64.8	56.5	59.5	68.0	71.4	75.0
Business awareness	62.5	73.9	59.5	65.3	64.3	50.0
Computing skills	59.3	52.2	54.8	66.7	47.6	68.8
Self-reliance	54.2	73.9	40.5	52.0	57.1	62.5
A-level grades	53.7	65.2	52.4	50.7	59.5	25.0
Course content	38.4	30.4	47.6	38.7	26.2	75.0
Sandwich course	31.5	34.8	35.7	38.7	28.6	18.8
Gap year (paid work)	31.0	30.4	40.5	26.7	28.6	37.5
Sport & hobbies	27.3	26.1	28.6	25.3	35.7	18.8

Second language	22.7	13.0	38.1	21.3	28.6	6.3
Gap year (voluntary/unpaid work)	21.3	21.7	28.6	14.7	23.8	25.0
GCSE grades	17.1	13.0	19.0	13.3	19.0	6.3
Gap year (travel)	12.5	8.7	23.8	8.0	16.7	6.3

Again, we have highlighted a few interesting results:

- Northern recruiters value self-reliance far more than the others, particularly their counterparts in the Midlands.

- Taking time out to travel is valued relatively highly in the Midlands, as is having a second language. The latter position contrasts with that in Scotland where having a second language scores surprisingly low.

- Londoners appear to be living by the 'work-hard-play-hard' adage, particularly keen as they are on both work experience *and* sport and hobbies.

HE AND ME

Just as important as the qualities recruiters expect and like to see in you is what they think of you. Before you even walk into an interview or assessment centre your potential recruiter will already have arrived at an opinion of you – an opinion formed by their perception of graduates in general as well as the content of your application/CV. It is unfortunate that you can spend all the time and effort in the world developing and demonstrating your employability only to fall foul of an idiosyncratic dislike for your university or for this year's crop of new graduates. It is important to be aware of how recruiters regard higher education and its output if you are to make informed study choices.

It is with this in mind that we consider Tables 7.4, 7.5 and 7.6.

TABLE 7.4 INFLUENCES OF A UNIVERSITY'S REPUTATION ON RECRUITERS' PERCEPTIONS OF GRADUATE EMPLOYABILITY

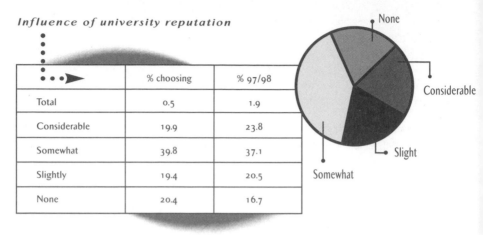

Influence of university reputation

	% choosing	% 97/98
Total	0.5	1.9
Considerable	19.9	23.8
Somewhat	39.8	37.1
Slightly	19.4	20.5
None	20.4	16.7

Table 7.4 indicates the extent to which recruiters are influenced by the reputation of a graduate's university or college when considering their employability. We have already surmised that the higher education institution you attend makes a difference to your subsequent employment prospects; the data presented here supports this.

Although only very few recruiters (0.5 per cent) were *totally* influenced by an applicant's university or college, the majority (about 60 per cent) were at least somewhat influenced. Only a fifth (20.4 per cent) claimed not to be influenced at all, only slightly more than were considerably so (19.9 per cent).

But even if you are fortunate enough to attend a university with a positive reputation you may still find that you are fighting an uphill battle against recruiters' opinions of graduates in general.

TABLE 7.5 RECRUITERS' PERCEPTIONS OF DEGREE STANDARDS

Perception of degree standards

	% choosing	% 98/99
Falling	13.4	21.1
Falling slightly	39.3	31.6
No change	40.3	38.2
Rising slightly	7.0	7.9
Rising	0.0	1.3

Whether they are creating or believing the hype, Table 7.5 reveals that graduate recruiters do not think too highly of the way degree standards are going. Almost all (93 per cent) believe that degrees are *not* getting any harder, and while 40.3 per cent think there has been no change of late, more than half (52.7 per cent) are of the opinion that standards are indeed falling or falling slightly.

Despite this apparent lack of faith in modern degrees, recruiters remain satisfied with the quality of the graduates they employ. Table 7.6 indicates that almost 80 per cent of recruiters rate new graduate employability as fairly good or good, and absolutely no one thinks of it as being poor.

TABLE 7.6 RECRUITERS' PERCEPTIONS OF NEW GRADUATES' EMPLOYABILITY

Perception of new graduate employability

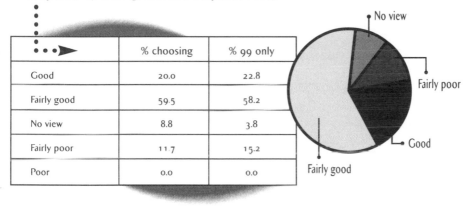

	% choosing	% 99 only
Good	20.0	22.8
Fairly good	59.5	58.2
No view	8.8	3.8
Fairly poor	11.7	15.2
Poor	0.0	0.0

There is probably not much you can do about recruiters' feelings on these matters, except perhaps prove them wrong. You can, however, use them to your best advantage by tailoring your choices and applications to match what they like. For instance, by emphasising your transferable skills and qualities on your applications and at interviews as well as your degree itself, you can shift the focus from falling educational standards and instead place it on new graduate employability.

And, of course, you can choose to attend a university or college that will serve you well *after* graduation . . .

8. Which Universities Produce the Most Employable Graduates?

Right now, it might seem as if you need to decide which university to *go to*; but for the rest of your life it will be more a case of the university you *come from*. And as we have seen, at no time is this more true than in the new graduate job market. Our evidence suggests that as many as four out of five recruiters are in some way influenced by the reputation of a graduate's university or college. And, more importantly, we have also found that such reputations vary according to subject.

And so we come to our subject tables – the most important part of this book. This is where all the thoughts and ideas we have been exploring thus far are put into practice. The information that follows will help you make the informed choices necessary to aid you in making the most of your investment in higher education by becoming the most employable graduate going.

BACKGROUND TO THE SUBJECT TABLES

The subject tables presented here are the result of a number of surveys of graduate recruiters' opinions that we have been carrying out for the last 12 years. Over this time we have repeatedly found that the definitions of a typical recruiter and an ideal graduate depend a great deal on the subject area in which the recruitment takes place. The specific employability qualities that recruiters look for in, say, an engineering graduate, are not exactly the same as for linguists, which in turn differ from mathematicians and so on. Similarly, different universities have their own reputations for producing employable graduates in each subject area.

The bulk of our research, therefore, focuses on how recruiters' views on employability and university reputation vary according to the subjects they recruit in.

The opinions that employers have expressed regarding higher education, graduates and employability qualities in general are only used to generate the subject tables if they come from participants who are actively recruiting one or more graduates from that subject area during the survey year. For example, the first four science tables are the result of only those responses coming from recruiters who have indicated their intention to recruit at least one science graduate in the coming year.

Recruiters also cast 'votes' for the institutions they feel produce graduates of above or below average employability (*positive* and *negative* respectively), according to subject area. (A list of the institutions recruiters have to choose from can be found in the appendices.) These votes are used as the basis for the institution rankings in each subject.

INTERPRETING THE SUBJECT TABLES

The subject tables should be relatively straightforward and easy to read. However, a helping hand is always welcome and we are happy to provide one. First, as we did for *all* recruiters on pages 37–43, we consider the subject-specific recruiters' perceptions of higher education and graduates in general:

Influence of university reputation

This table indicates the proportions of recruiters active in each subject that are 'totally', 'considerably', 'somewhat', 'slightly' or 'not' influenced by a university or college's reputation. It also compares the subject-specific results to the general case first shown on page 42.

Changing degree standards

Similarly, this table compares the subject-specific recruiters' opinions of degree standards with those of *all* recruiters – i.e. whether they think they are 'falling', 'falling slightly', 'not changing', 'rising slightly' or 'rising'.

New graduates' employability

Finally, we have the proportions of recruiters (both in each subject and generally) that rate new graduates' employability as 'good', 'fairly good', 'fairly poor' or 'poor'. They may also have 'no view' on the matter.

Then we examine how the employers who actively recruit in each subject area vary in their preferences for the skills, attributes and qualities that make a graduate employable:

Preferences for employability qualities

This table and accompanying bar chart illustrate the relative preferences recruiters in each subject group have for the employability qualities, skills and attributes first introduced in Table 7.1 and Figure 7.11 on page 37. The percentages within the table represent the proportions of recruiters that regard each quality as 'adding to the employability of a graduate'. Again the figures for *all* recruiters are included for comparison.

The bar chart should provide a clearer sense of how for each subject the most popular qualities vary from the norm.

Next we get into the real business of looking at how the participating recruiters perceive each university in terms of the employability of the graduates they produce:

Ranking of universities by employability points

The ranking presented here shows us which universities recruiters think produce the most employable graduates in each subject area.

We have awarded each university an employability score based on the positive and negative votes they received from recruiters in our survey. If a positive vote came from a recruiter actively recruiting in that subject area during the survey year then that institution was awarded *two* employability points. A vote from a non-active recruiter, on the other hand, is only worth *one* point.

Universities are ranked first according to the number of points they receive, from highest to lowest – i.e. the most preferred institution at number one, the least preferred at the bottom. In the event of more than one university receiving the same number of points, the one with the best vote difference (positive votes minus negative votes) is ranked highest. If they are still tied then the university with the fewest negative votes is placed first. If there is no such clear distinction, the tied universities are awarded equal ranking and listed in alphabetical order.

The risers and fallers

It is often interesting to see how different universities' fortunes change over time. In this case we have picked out the ten institutions that have risen through the ranking the most in the last three years, and the ten that have fallen the most. The tables show each riser and faller's rank this year, their rank in 1998 and the number of places in the employability ranking they have risen.

Ranking of universities by value-added

While it is important to see which universities recruiters prefer their graduate employees to come from, the main points rankings as presented above are not necessarily helpful or relevant to everyone that reads them. It is easy to recommend that a student interested in studying law should look into attending Oxford, Cambridge or the London School of Economics because they are rated by employers as the top three producers of employable law graduates. But that student may not realistically expect to meet the strict entry requirements that these institutions, and others like them, impose. For many students like this, indeed the *average* student, it would be useful to see how well perceived universities are, *relative to their entry requirements*. This is why we developed our measure of 'value-added'.

'Value-added' is an indication of a university's success in maintaining or enhancing a student's status over the time they spend studying for a degree. For example, two different universities taking two students with *very different* A-level or Scottish Highers grades go on to turn them into two graduates of the *same* standard of employability. In this case we can argue that the 'value' that has been added to each student during their time in higher education is defined by which university they attended. It follows that universities with a *higher* value-added score will make relatively *more* of their students' potential than those with a low score.

In calculating a value-added score for each university, we take the number of points it received in our survey as a measure of the employability of its graduates. To approximate the relative standing of students entering each university, we use the expected entry requirements for a single reference course in each subject – e.g. for *Civil Engineering/Construction* we use each university's entry requirements for the course *H200 Civil Engineering* (reference courses are chosen as typical courses that are provided by many universities – a list of which can be found in the appendices). This means that we *only* include universities that offer the specific reference course in our value-added rankings, resulting in cases where institutions ranked in the main table do not appear in its value-added equivalent, and vice versa. The difference between the final employability score and the entry requirements provides us with a raw measure of value-added.

To find out the *relative* value-added by each institution in each subject area, we then subtract this raw measure from the *average* raw measure across all institutions. The result is the final value-added figure used in our rankings.

For example, a university expecting 18 UCAS points* on entry and achieving 11 employability points on graduation has experienced a fall of seven points. If the average fall in that particular subject area is 6 points, then that university has experienced a fall *1 point worse* than average. Its value-added is therefore −1.

Further comments and selected quotes

Throughout the tables, we pick out and comment on a few interesting points and results. If anything of interest is not apparent from looking at the tables, we include it here. We also include a selection of quotes taken directly from recruiters' responses to our questionnaire.

Our comments are arbitrary and represent *only* what we find immediately eye-catching. They are kept to a minimum. You should look to draw your own conclusions, according to your own circumstances, at all times. This is what researching your degree should be all about – getting away from general opinion and giving thought to what course of action is best for *you*.

NB Results are from survey participants' votes, are not views of the authors or publisher and might not indicate quality, lack of it, or even actual provision of the subject/service. An individual's ability usually matters more than rankings.

---

* We use the *old* UCAS points tariff – see *NOTES AND WARNINGS* in the appendices.

9. The Subjects

BUSINESS AND MANAGEMENT

Employability rankings summary

Total votes: 360
Universities ranked: 96   **Not ranked:** 1
Highest: Warwick (28 points)   **Lowest:** Luton (-6 points)

Recruiters' perceptions of higher education and graduates

Influence of university reputation

	Business %	All replies %
Total	0.0	0.5
Considerable	16.7	19.9
Somewhat	38.9	39.8
Slight	25.9	19.4
None	18.5	20.4

Over half (55.6 per cent) of recruiters of business and management graduates are at least somewhat influenced by universities' reputations, and a further 25.9 per cent are slightly so. Unlike some other subjects, this is fairly similar to the general case.

Changing degree standards

	Business %	All replies %
Falling	12.5	13.4
Falling slightly	30.4	39.3
No change	53.6	40.3
Rising slightly	3.6	7.0
Rising	0.0	0.0

While perceptions of degree standards are again close to the average, there is more of a leaning towards there being no change with more than half (53.6 per cent) of recruiters choosing that option. However, there are still very few who actually believe degrees are getting harder so you are not likely to benefit from graduating more recently.

New graduates' employability

	Business %	All replies %
Good	17.5	20.0
Fairly good	61.4	59.5
No view	5.3	8.8
Fairly poor	15.8	11.7
Poor	0.0	0.0

More encouraging is the fact that almost 80 per cent of business and management recruiters rate new graduates' employability as being either fairly good or good, although a slightly higher proportion think it is fairly poor than in general.

Preferences for employability qualities

Rank	Employability qualities	Business %	All replies %
1=	Verbal communication skills	83.3	83.8
1=	Enthusiasm	83.3	81.5
3	Teamworking	80.0	66.7
4=	Personal/transferable skills	76.7	66.7
4=	Work experience	76.7	69.9
6	Business awareness	75.0	62.5
7=	Written communication skills	73.3	71.8
7=	Numeracy	73.3	64.8
9	Problem solving	70.6	66.9
10	Self-reliance	66.7	54.2
11	Degree classification	63.3	67.6
12	Computing skills	60.0	59.3
13	A-level grades	56.7	53.7
14	Sandwich course	40.0	31.5
15	Course content	38.3	38.4

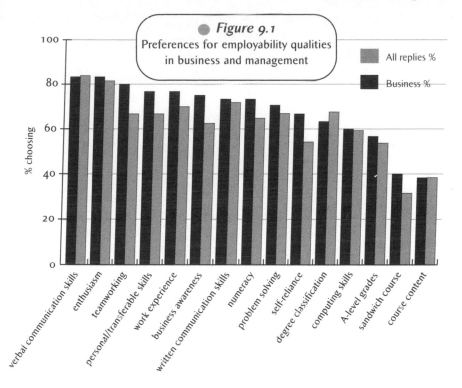

Figure 9.1
Preferences for employability qualities in business and management

Verbal communication skills and enthusiasm maintain their ownership of the top two places of this list, but written communication falls from third generally to equal seventh here. Unsurprisingly, business awareness does relatively well, and the qualities that you would associate with a generic business environment – e.g. teamworking, personal/transferable skills, self-reliance, work experience – understandably also make their mark.

RANKING OF UNIVERSITIES
BY EMPLOYABILITY POINTS ••••

Rank	University	Employability points
1	Warwick	28
2=	Leeds	18
2=	Nottingham	18
4=	Aston	17
4=	Manchester	17
6	Bath	17
7	Birmingham	15
8=	Bristol	12
8=	Cambridge	12
10	Oxford	12
11=	Hull	11
11=	Leeds Metropolitan	11
13	Lancaster	11
14	London School of Economics	10
15	Loughborough	10
16	Brighton	9
17=	Kingston	9
17=	Southampton	9
19	UMIST	8
20=	Oxford Brookes	8
20=	Sheffield	8
22=	Exeter	7
22=	University College London	7
24	Bournemouth	7
25=	Durham	7
25=	Plymouth	7
25=	Reading	7
25=	University of Wales Cardiff	7
29	Nottingham Trent	7
30=	Belfast	6
30=	Edinburgh	6
30=	Essex	6
30=	Portsmouth	6
34	Liverpool John Moores	6
35=	Liverpool	5
35=	Imperial College London	5
35=	Surrey	5
38=	De Montfort	5
38=	Huddersfield	5
40	Newcastle upon Tyne	4
41	University of Wales Bangor	4
42	Brunel	4
43=	Salford	3
43=	Sheffield Hallam	3
46=	Bradford	3
46=	City	3
46=	Coventry	3
46=	Strathclyde	3
46=	York	3
48=	Kings College London	3
51=	Abertay	2

Rank	University	Employability points
51=	Keele	2
51=	Kent	2
51=	Leicester	2
51=	Queen Mary & Westfield College London	2
51=	Sussex	2
51=	Westminster	2
58=	Manchester Metropolitan	2
58=	University of Wales Swansea	2
60	West of England	2
61	Thames Valley	2
62	Stirling	1
63=	Anglia Polytechnic University	1
63=	Heriot-Watt	1
65	Northumbria	1
66=	Glasgow	0
66=	Ulster	0
68=	Central England	-1
68=	Glasgow Caledonian	-1
68=	Goldsmiths College London	-1
68=	Napier	-1
72	Hertfordshire	-1
73=	Central Lancashire	-2
73=	Dundee	-2
73=	East Anglia	-2
73=	Glamorgan	-2
73=	Greenwich	-2
73=	Lincoln	-2
73=	Royal Holloway College	-2
73=	Paisley	-2
73=	Robert Gordon	-2
73=	St Andrews	-2
73=	South Bank	-2
73=	University of Wales Aberystwyth	-2
73=	University of Wales Lampeter	-2
73=	Wolverhampton	-2
87	Middlesex	-3
88=	Buckingham	-3
88=	Derby	-3
88=	Sunderland	-3
88=	Teesside	-3
92=	East London	-4
92=	London Guildhall	-4
92=	Staffordshire	-4
95	North London	-6
96	Luton	-6

The risers and fallers

TOP TEN RISERS

Rank 2002	University	Rank 1998	Change
20=	Oxford Brookes	87	67 ▲
41	University of Wales Bangor	81=	40 ▲
38=	De Montfort	76=	38 ▲
30=	Essex	67	37 ▲
30=	Portsmouth	61=	31 ▲
24	Bournemouth	54=	30 ▲
25=	University of Wales Cardiff	52=	27 ▲
10	Oxford	36	26 ▲
16	Brighton	41	25 ▲
51=	Westminster	76=	25 ▲

'TOP' TEN FALLERS

Rank 2002	University	Rank 1998	Change
65	Northumbria	38	27 ▼
73=	Dundee	43=	30 ▼
46=	Strathclyde	16	30 ▼
46=	Bradford	15	31 ▼
43=	Sheffield Hallam	10	33 ▼
58=	Manchester Metropolitan	20	38 ▼
73=	St Andrews	30=	43 ▼
62	Stirling	17=	45 ▼
63=	Heriot-Watt	12	51 ▼
66=	Glasgow	11	55 ▼

The well-established universities filling out the top ten dominate the main list but their newer cousins are starting to snap at their heels a bit. Former polytechnics Leeds Metropolitan, Brighton and Kingston all take a place in the top 20 while others such as De Montfort and Oxford Brookes in particular put on good performances in the top ten risers. It appears that Scottish universities are falling away somewhat with no fewer than six institutions among the ten biggest fallers in business and management.

RANKING OF UNIVERSITIES BY VALUE-ADDED

Rank	University	Value Added (ave=0)
1	Leeds Metropolitan	10
2	Thames Valley	9
3	Manchester	8
4	Brighton	6
5=	Abertay	5
5=	Kingston	5
7=	Anglia Polytechnic University	4
7=	Bournemouth	4
7=	Huddersfield	4
7=	Liverpool John Moores	4
7=	Plymouth	4
12=	Kent	3
12=	Portsmouth	3
14=	Coventry	2
14=	De Montfort	2
14=	Hull	2
14=	Nottingham Trent	2
18=	Glamorgan	1
18=	Lincoln	1
18=	South Bank	1
21	Teesside	0
22=	East London	-1
22=	Greenwich	-1
22=	London Guildhall	-1
22=	Salford	-1

Rank	University	Value Added (ave=0)
22=	West of England	-1
27=	Bradford	-2
27=	Buckingham	-2
27=	Central England	-2
27=	Derby	-2
27=	Liverpool	-2
27=	Middlesex	-2
33=	Brunel	-3
33=	Manchester Metropolitan	-3
33=	Sheffield	-3
36	Glasgow Caledonian	-4
37=	Central Lancashire	-5
37=	Edinburgh	-5
37=	Hertfordshire	-5
37=	Luton	-5
37=	North London	-5
37=	Robert Gordon	-5
37=	Staffordshire	-5
37=	Westminster	-5
45=	Stirling	-6
45=	Sunderland	-6
47=	Ulster	-7
47=	University of Wales Swansea	-7
49	City	-8

NOTE Value-added calculations are based on the single reference course Business N120. Only institutions offering this course are ranked.

Leeds Metropolitan adds to its good showing in the main ranking by topping the value-added table. In fact, in contrast to the points ranking, the new universities and former polytechnics feature heavily in the top 20 value-adding institutions. Of particular interest is Thames Valley University, which makes light of being ranked as low as 61 in the main table by achieving second position here with a respectable value-added score of nine.

Further comments and selected quotes

Warwick's number one ranking is their first in any of our surveys in any subject. Several recruiters mentioned them as being *'especially targeted'*. One major London firm, who voted for Warwick in business and management, added that they provide *'good graduates in many disciplines'*.

Despite **Oxford Brookes**'s dramatic surge up the rankings, it is still out-scored by three other former polytechnics: **Kingston** (17th equal), **Brighton** (16th) and **Leeds Metropolitan** (11th equal). The latter is in fact the highest-ever ranking by any ex-poly.

North London and **Luton** do particularly badly out of the survey. Occupying the bottom two places in the main ranking, they also appear in the bottom half of the value-added table. And one recruiter from the South-East, while being only slightly influenced by a graduate's university, comments that she has *'seen a number of applicants (from Luton) but none meeting our standards'.*

Leeds does well by progressing to number two on points, though one local firm describes their graduates as *'variable'*. Leeds' position owes much to a surge of support for their business graduates in the first of the three surveys that make up the 2001 results. Our methodology means that this support will not be included again next year.

Expected entry requirements for Business (N120) at **City**, which lies 49th and last in the value-added list, are approximately the same as at **Manchester**, which comes in at number three!

A number of specialist management courses received favourable comments. One property firm praises **'Land Management'** at **Reading**, while another recruiter in the Midlands likes the 'relevance of **Manufacturing Management'** at **Nottingham**.

One household name recruiter favours the two Nottingham universities for business graduates. **Nottingham** rises to equal second and **Nottingham Trent** to 29th, the latter having the edge in terms of value-added. Keeping within the East Midlands, the same recruiter *'particularly avoids'* Derby's graduates.

Finally, one medium-sized company, currently recruiting business graduates, seems to have a very bleak outlook, believing degree standards to be falling, new graduates' suitability for work as fairly poor and that *'there are more capable people now than ten years ago, but more inadequate graduates'.*

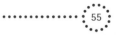

CIVIL ENGINEERING/CONSTRUCTION

Employability rankings summary

Total votes: 213
Universities ranked: 72   **Not ranked:** 25
Highest: Loughborough (18 points)   **Lowest:** South Bank (-8 points)

Recruiters' perceptions of higher education and graduates

Influence of university reputation

	Civ Eng/Construction %	All replies %
Total	0.0	0.5
Considerable	25.0	19.9
Somewhat	53.1	39.8
Slight	18.8	19.4
None	3.1	20.4

Although none chose 'Total', it is noticeable that in this case the results are more skewed towards the reputation of a university having a considerable influence on recruiters' perceptions of graduates than in general. It would seem, therefore, that recruiters of civil engineering and construction graduates are more likely to take the university you attend into account.

Changing degree standards

	Civ Eng/Construction %	All replies %
Falling	12.5	13.4
Falling slightly	43.8	39.3
No change	34.4	40.3
Rising slightly	9.4	7.0
Rising	0.0	0.0

The results here are broadly similar to the average. Just over half the civil engineering and construction recruiters that responded believed degree standards are either falling or

falling slightly. On the plus side, however, nearly a tenth thought that standards were actually rising slightly. This disparity might be a result of differences in individual courses.

New graduates' employability

	Civ Eng/Construction %	All replies %
Good	25.8	20.0
Fairly good	48.4	59.5
No view	6.5	8.8
Fairly poor	19.4	11.7
Poor	0.0	0.0

Again, the subject specific results are similar to the overall findings. The general opinion seems to be that civil engineering and construction graduates exhibit good employment skills. Almost three in four recruiters regarded their candidates' employability as being good or fairly good.

Preferences for employability qualities

Rank	Employability qualities	Civ Eng/Construction %	All replies %
1=	Verbal communication skills	87.9	83.8
1=	Enthusiasm	87.9	81.5
3	Degree classification	81.0	67.6
4	Work experience	78.8	69.9
5	Teamworking	75.8	66.7
6=	Written communication skills	72.7	71.8
6=	Numeracy	72.7	64.8
8	Problem solving	71.4	66.9
9	Course content	69.7	38.4
10	Computing skills	66.7	59.3
11=	Personal/transferable skills	63.6	66.7
11=	Self-reliance	63.6	54.2
13=	A-level grades	54.5	53.7
13=	Business awareness	54.5	62.5
15=	Sandwich course	42.4	31.5
15=	Gap year (paid employment)	42.4	31.5

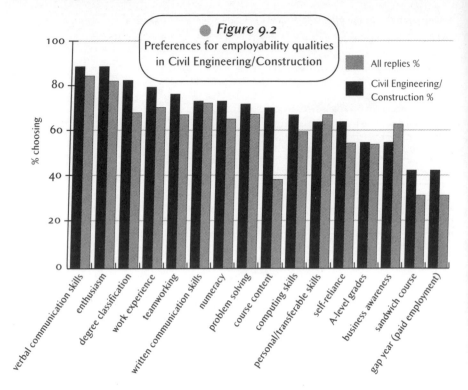

● *Figure 9.2*
Preferences for employability qualities in Civil Engineering/Construction

All replies %

Civil Engineering/Construction %

Perhaps as a result of the strong vocational element of civil engineering and construction courses it seems as though the characteristics of your degree are significant in the eyes of prospective employers. This is in keeping with the previous table which pointed out that civil engineering and construction recruiters take greater heed of the idiosyncrasies of a degree than do the average – degree classification, sandwich course and, in particular, course content standing out from the crowd. Therefore, to enhance your employability you would be advised to take care in seeking out a course that employers hold in high regard.

RANKING OF UNIVERSITIES BY EMPLOYABILITY POINTS ••••

Rank	University	Employability points
1	Loughborough	18
2	Birmingham	13
3	University of Wales Cardiff	12
4	Leeds	11
5	Heriot-Watt	11
6=	Bath	10
6=	Sheffield	10
8	Surrey	9
9	UMIST	9
10=	Bristol	8
10=	Southampton	8
12	Nottingham	8
13	Manchester	7
14=	Edinburgh	7
14=	Newcastle upon Tyne	7
14=	Strathclyde	7
14=	Warwick	7
18	Portsmouth	7
19	Liverpool	6
20=	Durham	6
20=	Nottingham Trent	6
20=	Salford	6
23	Imperial College London	5
24=	Aberdeen	5
24=	Aston	5
24=	Exeter	5
24=	Plymouth	5
28=	Cambridge	4
28=	Oxford	4
28=	Sheffield Hallam	4
31	Brunel	3
32=	Coventry	3
32=	Leicester	3
32=	Kings College London	3
32=	Reading	3
32=	York	3

Rank	University	Employability points
37	Oxford Brookes	3
38=	Anglia Polytechnic University	2
38=	Belfast	2
38=	Central England	2
38=	City	2
38=	Dundee	2
38=	Greenwich	2
38=	Hull	2
38=	Kingston	2
38=	Liverpool John Moores	2
38=	University College London	2
38=	Teesside	2
38=	Ulster	2
38=	West of England	2
51=	Napier	2
51=	Paisley	2
53=	Glasgow	1
53=	Keele	1
53=	Lancaster	1
53=	London School of Economics	1
53=	Middlesex	1
53=	Stirling	1
53=	Sussex	1
53=	University of Wales Aberystwyth	1
53=	University of Wales Swansea	1
62	St Andrews	1
63=	Robert Gordon	0
63=	Wolverhampton	0
65=	Luton	-1
65=	Thames Valley	-1
67=	Buckingham	-2
67=	East London	-2
69=	Abertay	-2
69=	Glasgow Caledonian	-2
71	Brighton	-3
72	South Bank	-8

The risers and fallers

TOP TEN RISERS

Rank 2002	University	Rank 1998	Change
14=	Warwick	45=	31 ▲
8	Surrey	34=	26 ▲
24=	Plymouth	45=	21 ▲
38=	Liverpool John Moores	57	19 ▲
20=	Nottingham Trent	38=	18 ▲
20=	Salford	37	17 ▲
1	Loughborough	12=	11 ▲
9	UMIST	20	11 ▲
5	Heriot-Watt	15=	10 ▲
14=	Edinburgh	23=	9 ▲

'TOP' TEN FALLERS

Rank 2002	University	Rank 1998	Change
67=	Buckingham/East London	45=	22 ▼
28=	Oxford	6	22 ▼
38=	Belfast	15=	23 ▼
69=	Abertay	45=	24 ▼
71	Brighton	45=	26 ▼
72	South Bank	45=	27 ▼
53=	London School of Economics	26=	27 ▼
28=	Cambridge	1	27 ▼
53=	Glasgow	21=	32 ▼
62	St Andrews	26=	36 ▼

Oh, how are the mighty fallen! The relatively poor performances of Oxford and Cambridge Universities in this year's survey are nothing if not striking. It is possible that there is an element of complacency creeping into the old universities, but it is more likely that their relative decline (there weren't actually any votes cast against Oxbridge in this subject), and the rise of institutions like Liverpool John Moores, Nottingham Trent and Salford, is down to recruiters broadening their horizons and considering graduates of the newer universities.

RANKING OF UNIVERSITIES BY VALUE-ADDED

Rank	University	Value Added (ave=0)
1	Loughborough	14
2	Napier	8
3=	Heriot-Watt	7
3=	Leeds	7
5=	Glasgow Caledonian	6
5=	Nottingham Trent	6
7=	Birmingham	5
7=	Surrey	5
7=	University of Wales Cardiff	5
10=	Bradford	4
10=	Paisley	4
12=	Manchester	3
12=	Plymouth	3
12=	University of Wales Swansea	3
15=	Leeds Metropolitan	2
15=	Salford	2
17=	Aston	1
17=	Edinburgh	1
17=	Exeter	1
17=	UMIST	1
17=	Newcastle upon Tyne	1
17=	Strathclyde	1
17=	Warwick	1
24=	Glamorgan	0
24=	Hertfordshire	0

Rank	University	Value Added (ave=0)
24=	Liverpool	0
24=	Portsmouth	0
24=	Sheffield	0
24=	Sheffield Hallam	0
24=	Southampton	0
24=	Wolverhampton	0
32=	Coventry	-1
32=	Nottingham	-1
32=	Oxford Brookes	-1
35=	Abertay	-2
35=	Bristol	-2
35=	City	-2
35=	Dundee	-2
35=	Greenwich	-2
35=	Kingston	-2
35=	Liverpool John Moores	-2
42=	Aberdeen	-3
42=	Glasgow	-3
44=	Durham	-4
44=	University College London	-4
46	Ulster	-5
47	East London	-6
48	Oxford	10
49	South Bank	-12
50	Brighton	-13

NOTE Value-added calculations are based on the single reference course Civil Engineering I1200. Only institutions offering this course are ranked.

Again, Loughborough comes out on top by quite a margin, indicating that it is *the* place to go if you want to make the most of your potential. The good showing of lower-ranked universities Napier, Glasgow Caledonian and Paisley suggests that although such institutions may not necessarily provide absolutely the 'best' graduates, they are, for many, still a good option.

Further comments and selected quotes

For the second year running, **Loughborough** claims top spot as the employers' favourite provider of civil engineering and construction graduates. It would seem that Loughborough also adds the greatest value to its graduates, meaning that students achieving average A-level results can make the most of themselves by studying there.

One London company indicated that they *'communicate with only a select number of universities'* but include Loughborough among them because of *'course content and communication with staff'*. All in all, it has been another good year for our friends in north Leicestershire.

Nevertheless, Loughborough's progress from 12th in 1998 to first in the latest table is clearly overshadowed by **Warwick's** rise of 31 places. **Surrey, Plymouth** and **Nottingham Trent** also do well on this front, possibly because, as one major South-of-England-based recruiter said about the latter, *'they care for their students and what happens to them'.*

Despite this praise, both Nottingham Trent and Plymouth are overtaken by **Portsmouth** as the best-placed former polytechnic in this subject.

Imperial College London's decline of 21 places only just avoids a place in the 'top' ten fallers but coincides with one employer's view that they (and **UMIST**) *'train civil engineers as consultants not contractors'.*

One London-based recruiter admitted that she tends *'not to interview from the ex-polytechnics'* claiming that it is *'more difficult for their graduates to qualify in the profession'.*

For the third year running **Brighton** takes quite a fall: 45th equal in 1998 and 57th equal last year, it now finds itself 71st, just one place from the bottom. One recruiter voted against *both* Brighton and its partner in crime at the bottom **South Bank**, and a small company in the South East complained that these two universities' graduates *'lack understanding of the basics'.*

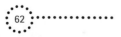

COMPUTING/IT

Employability rankings summary

Total votes: 256
Universities ranked: 77   **Not ranked:** 20
Highest: UMIST (29 points)   **Lowest:** Oxford Brookes (-2 points)

Recruiters' perceptions of higher education and graduates

Influence of university reputation

	Computing %	All replies %
Total	1.6	0.5
Considerable	14.5	19.9
Somewhat	45.2	39.8
Slight	21.0	19.4
None	17.7	20.4

This is one of the occasional cases where a small percentage of recruiters have admitted to being *totally* influenced by a university's reputation. 1.6 per cent may not be much but it is noteworthy considering that for most subjects absolutely no one chooses this option.
Other than this, the case for computing/IT is largely similar to the average with just over 60 per cent of recruiters acknowledging that university reputation sways their decisions at least somewhat.

Changing degree standards

	Computing %	All replies %
Falling	9.4	13.4
Falling slightly	35.9	39.3
No change	48.4	40.3
Rising slightly	6.3	7.0
Rising	0.0	0.0

Again, the results for computing/IT are not much different from those for all subjects combined. If anything, recruiters of computing and IT graduates are more neutral towards changing degree standards than average, almost half believing that there has been no change of late. Those who think that standards are actually rising are in a very small minority.

New graduates' employability

	Computing %	All replies %
Good	18.9	20.0
Fairly good	64.1	59.5
No view	7.8	8.8
Fairly poor	9.4	11.7
Poor	0.0	0.0

Slightly more than four in five computing/IT recruiters currently regard the standard of new graduate employability as being fairly good or good. This closely reflects their reassuring opinion of graduates in general. There are, however, approximately 10 per cent who think new graduate employability is fairly poor, so there is little room for complacency.

Preferences for employability qualities

Rank	Employability qualities	Computing %	All replies %
1 =	Computing skills	81.8	59.3
1 =	Enthusiasm	81.8	81.5
3	Verbal communication skills	77.3	83.8
4	Problem solving	76.3	66.9
5 =	Work experience	72.7	69.9
5 =	Written communication skills	72.7	71.8
7	Teamworking	71.2	66.7
8	Business awareness	68.2	62.5
9	Degree classification	66.7	67.6
10	Numeracy	65.2	64.8
11	Personal/transferable skills	63.6	66.7
12	Self-reliance	56.1	54.2
13	A-level grades	53.0	53.7
14	Course content	50.0	38.4
15	Sandwich course	39.4	31.5

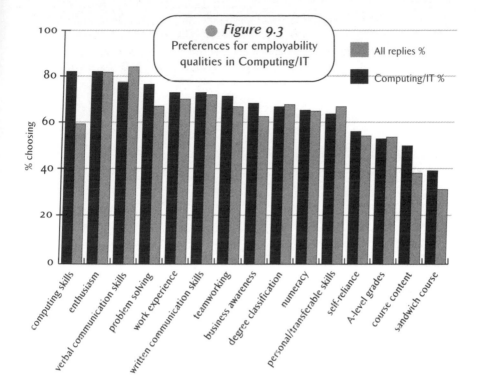

Figure 9.3
Preferences for employability qualities in Computing/IT

■ All replies %
■ Computing/IT %

It is no big surprise to see computing skills make a massive leap to the top of the tree here. While the generic graduate who boasts a bit of computer literacy is not a special case any more, it is essential that computing and IT graduates can display the more advanced forms of computing skills. Other notable results are the relatively high levels of endorsement for problem solving and course content. It is understandable in an industry built on finding quicker and more effective ways of conducting business that the former proves popular, while the latter's recognition probably reflects the direct relevance of computing and IT courses to subsequent jobs. And it may not come as a surprise to anyone who has attempted to report a problem to IT technical support that verbal communication skills are seen as relatively less important here!

RANKING OF UNIVERSITIES BY EMPLOYABILITY POINTS ••••

Rank	University	Employability points
1	UMIST	29
2	Cambridge	22
3=	Birmingham	20
3=	Bristol	20
3=	Manchester	20
6	Aston	18
7=	Imperial College London	17
7=	Warwick	17
9=	Brunel	14
9=	Edinburgh	14
11	Nottingham	13
12=	Leeds	10
12=	Oxford	10
12=	York	10
15	Sheffield	10
16	Southampton	9
17	De Montfort	8
18=	Bath	8
18=	Glasgow	8
18=	Heriot-Watt	8
18=	Reading	8
18=	Strathclyde	8
23=	Durham	6
23=	University College London	6
23=	Loughborough	6
23=	Staffordshire	6
23=	University of Wales Cardiff	6
23=	West of England	6
29=	Kings College London	5
29=	Newcastle upon Tyne	5
29=	Nottingham Trent	5
29=	Sheffield Hallam	5
33=	Liverpool	4
33=	Liverpool John Moores	4
33=	Ulster	4
33=	Westminster	4
37=	London School of Economics	3
37=	Portsmouth	3
39	Manchester Metropolitan	3

Rank	University	Employability points
40=	Aberdeen	2
40=	Abertay	2
40=	Belfast	2
40=	Bournemouth	2
40=	City	2
40=	Coventry	2
40=	Derby	2
40=	Dundee	2
40=	Glamorgan	2
40=	Kent	2
40=	Lancaster	2
40=	Middlesex	2
40=	Napier	2
40=	Northumbria	2
40=	Paisley	2
40=	Plymouth	2
40=	St Andrews	2
40=	Sunderland	2
40=	Surrey	2
40=	University of Wales Aberystwyth	2
40=	Wolverhampton	2
61=	Central England	1
61=	Exeter	1
61=	Hull	1
61=	Sussex	1
61=	University of Wales Swansea	1
66	Kingston	1
67=	Bradford	0
67=	Leeds Metropolitan	0
69	Hertfordshire	0
70=	East Anglia	-2
70=	East London	-2
70=	Queen Mary & Westfield College London	-2
70=	Luton	-2
70=	South Bank	-2
70=	Teesside	-2
70=	Thames Valley	-2
77	Oxford Brookes	-2

The risers and fallers

TOP TEN RISERS

Rank 2002	University	Rank 1998	Change
17	De Montfort	67=	50 ▲
23=	Durham	61	38 ▲
33=	Westminster	63	30 ▲
6	Aston	33=	27 ▲
3=	Bristol	30	27 ▲
40=	Derby	67=	27 ▲
29=	Kings College London	52=	23 ▲
29=	Sheffield Hallam	52=	23 ▲
33=	Liverpool John Moores	52=	19 ▲
23=	West of England	39=	16 ▲

'TOP' TEN FALLERS

Rank 2002	University	Rank 1998	Change
70=	Queen Mary & Westfield College London	52=	18 ▼
70=	South Bank	52=	18 ▼
40=	Aberdeen	20=	20 ▼
40=	Napier	20=	20 ▼
67=	Bradford	39=	28 ▼
61=	Sussex	31=	30 ▼
70=	Teesside	39=	31 ▼
66	Kingston	17=	39 ▼
69	Hertfordshire	14=	45 ▼
61=	Exeter	15=	46 ▼

Perhaps surprisingly for a relatively new subject area, the old universities once again feature heavily in the top ten. The likes of Cambridge, Bristol and Warwick are, however, outperformed by UMIST, which occupies the top spot, scoring an impressive 29 points. Overall, the results are positive for the computing and IT departments with only eight institutions receiving a negative score, and even then only just.

De Montfort University surges to the top of the risers list and becomes at number 17 the highest placed former polytechnic in the process. The rest of the top ten risers consist of a nice spread of old, new and ex-poly universities, perhaps reflecting how all institutions are developing the ways they deliver what is a youthful subject at a similar rate. The three biggest fallers – Kingston, Hertfordshire and Exeter – appear to have experienced a spectacular fall from grace, from the top 20 three years ago to the bottom 20 now.

RANKING OF UNIVERSITIES BY VALUE-ADDED

Rank	University	Value Added (ave=0)
1	UMIST	19
2=	Aston	10
2=	Birmingham	10
2=	Manchester	10
5=	Bristol	8
5=	Robert Gordon	8
5=	Staffordshire	8
8=	Cambridge	7
8=	De Montfort	7
10=	Abertay	6
10=	Edinburgh	6
10=	Glamorgan	6
10=	Heriot-Watt	6
10=	Napier	6
10=	Westminster	6
10=	Wolverhampton	6
17=	Brunel	5
17=	Greenwich	5
17=	Nottingham	5
20=	Anglia Polytechnic University	4
20=	Coventry	4
20=	Middlesex	4
20=	North London	4
20=	Paisley	4
20=	Plymouth	4
26=	Central England	3
26=	Warwick	3
28=	Buckingham	2
28=	Glasgow	2
28=	Lincoln	2
28=	Manchester Metropolitan	2
28=	Reading	2
28=	Strathclyde	2
28=	West of England	2
35	Imperial College London	1
36=	Aberdeen	0
36=	Central Lancashire	0
36=	East London	0
36=	Leeds	0
36=	Luton	0
36=	Sheffield	0

Rank	University	Value Added (ave=0)
42=	Nottingham Trent	-1
42=	Southampton	-1
44=	Bath	-2
44=	Huddersfield	-2
44=	Liverpool	-2
44=	Loughborough	-2
44=	Stirling	-2
44=	Sunderland	-2
44=	Teesside	-2
44=	Ulster	-2
44=	University of Wales Aberystwyth	-2
53=	Hertfordshire	-3
53=	Hull	-3
53=	Kingston	-3
53=	Newcastle upon Tyne	-3
53=	Portsmouth	-3
58=	Belfast	-4
58=	Bradford	-4
58=	Brighton	-4
58=	Durham	-4
58=	Keele	-4
58=	Lancaster	-4
58=	Oxford	-4
58=	St Andrews	-4
58=	Salford	-4
58=	University of Wales Bangor	-4
58=	University of Wales Cardiff	-4
58=	York	-4
70	Exeter	-5
71=	Essex	-6
71=	Kent	-6
71=	Leicester	-6
71=	University College London	-6
75	University of Wales Swansea	-7
76	City	-8
77=	East Anglia	-9
77=	Kings College London	-9
77=	Sussex	-9
80	Royal Holloway London	-10
81	Queen Mary & Westfield College London	-12

NOTE Value-added calculations are based on the single reference course Computing G500. Only institutions offering this course are ranked.

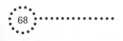

UMIST cements its position as the leading producer of employable computing and IT graduates by also topping our value-added ranking by quite a margin. Its expected entry requirements for Computing (G500) are the same as Queen Mary & Westfield's, which appears in 81st, and last, place. De Montfort repeats its strong showing in the main ranking by reaching eighth equal in value-added. Interestingly, despite demanding entry requirements, Cambridge joins UMIST and De Montfort in the top ten. Finally, the University of London seems not to be making the most of its computing and IT students: they have four institutions in the bottom eight.

Further comments and selected quotes

This is **UMIST**'s third successive year as the employers' number one in this subject. Since 1998 they have swapped places with **Cambridge**, now lying second.

Counting 2002 survey votes alone would see **Warwick** reach the top spot (remember that our results are based on the last three surveys). All but one of their supporters are currently active recruiters and include one from the South that speaks of Warwick's *'strong reputation for good IT students'*.

Several former polytechnics received noteworthy comments. **Kingston**, ranked 66th, is said to produce graduates with *'good breadth but poor depth of knowledge'* and **South Bank**, ranked 79th equal, is described as *'weak'* despite supplying *'lots of applicants'*. Conversely, a large Midlands organisation praises the *'excellent course, staff and work placement'* for computing at **Staffordshire** which rises to 23rd equal.

ELECTRICAL ENGINEERING/ELECTRONICS

Employability rankings summary

Total votes: 243
Universities ranked: 73   **Not ranked:** 24
Highest: UMIST (26 points)   **Lowest:** Liverpool John Moores (-4 points)

Recruiters' perceptions of higher education and graduates

Influence of university reputation

	Electrical Engineering %	All replies %
Total	0.0	0.5
Considerable	22.2	19.9
Somewhat	48.9	39.8
Slight	15.6	19.4
None	13.3	20.4

Recruiters of electrical engineering and electronics graduates are slightly more likely to take institution into account than average. More than 70 per cent are somewhat or considerably influenced by a graduate's university or college, while only 13.3 per cent are not influenced at all. Still, not a single recruiter owned up to being totally under the influence of reputation.

Changing degree standards

	Electrical Engineering %	All replies %
Falling	12.8	13.4
Falling slightly	38.3	39.3
No change	42.6	40.3
Rising slightly	6.4	7.0
Rising	0.0	0.0

Over half believe that degree standards are falling and only 6.4 per cent think the opposite. However, this is an almost identical set of results to the general case so there appears not to be anything peculiar in this respect about electrical engineering or electronics degrees.

New graduates' employability

	Electrical Engineering %	All replies %
Good	23.9	20.0
Fairly good	54.3	59.5
No view	10.9	8.8
Fairly poor	10.9	11.7
Poor	0.0	0.0

Again, the subject specific results are very similar to the general case. If anything, electrical engineering and electronics graduates are considered *more* employable, since a slightly bigger proportion of recruiters opted for 'good' over 'fairly good', but this is probably a negligible difference.

Preferences for employability qualities

Rank	Employability qualities	Electrical Engineering %	All replies %
1	Verbal communication skills	89.6	83.3
2	Enthusiasm	83.3	81.5
3=	Degree classification	79.2	67.6
3=	Work experience	79.2	69.9
5=	Written communication skills	72.9	71.8
5=	Numeracy	72.9	64.8
7	Teamworking	70.8	66.7
8	Problem solving	68.0	66.9
9=	Business awareness	66.7	62.5
9=	Personal/transferable skills	66.7	66.7
11	Computing skills	62.5	59.3
12=	A-level grades	56.3	53.7
12=	Course content	56.3	38.4
12=	Self-reliance	56.3	54.2
15	Sandwich course	52.1	31.5

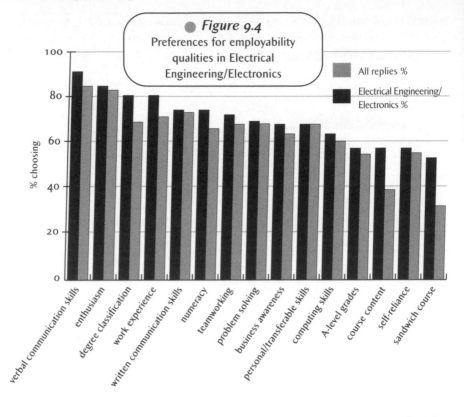

Figure 9.4
Preferences for employability qualities in Electrical Engineering/Electronics

All replies %

Electrical Engineering/ Electronics %

% choosing

verbal communication skills
enthusiasm
degree classification
work experience
written communication skills
numeracy
teamworking
problem solving
business awareness
personal/transferable skills
computing skills
A-level grades
course content
self-reliance
sandwich course

As we would expect for a largely vocational subject area such as this, where specific skills are more important, the four qualities that stand out as being more significant for electrical engineering and electronics graduates are degree classification, work experience, course content and sandwich course. Employers of electrical engineers would expect their new recruits to come armed with the relevant skills that are provided by good degree courses and work experience. However, while such qualities are relatively important in this subject, verbal communication and enthusiasm remain at the top.

RANKING OF UNIVERSITIES BY EMPLOYABILITY POINTS

Rank	University	Employability points
1	UMIST	26
2	Imperial College London	25
3	Birmingham	20
4	Brunel	18
5	Cambridge	17
6	Strathclyde	15
7=	Bristol	14
7=	Southampton	14
9	Heriot-Watt	14
10=	Nottingham	13
10=	Sheffield	13
12	Bath	12
13	Edinburgh	12
14	Belfast	11
15	Loughborough	10
16	Aston	10
17	Oxford	9
18	Warwick	8
19=	Hull	7
19=	Manchester	7
19=	York	7
22=	Glasgow	6
22=	Kings College London	6
22=	Portsmouth	6
25=	Durham	5
25=	Leeds	5
25=	Liverpool	5
25=	Plymouth	5
29=	Exeter	4
29=	Salford	4
29=	St Andrews	4
29=	Stirling	4
29=	University College London	4
29=	University of Wales Cardiff	4
35	Coventry	3
36	Nottingham Trent	3
37=	Aberdeen	2

Rank	University	Employability points
37=	Abertay	2
37=	Bradford	2
37=	Brighton	2
37=	Essex	2
37=	Glamorgan	2
37=	Hertfordshire	2
37=	Lancaster	2
37=	Manchester Metropolitan	2
37=	Napier	2
37=	Newcastle upon Tyne	2
37=	Paisley	2
37=	University of Wales Aberystwyth	2
37=	West of England	2
37=	Westminster	2
52=	Oxford Brookes	1
52=	Surrey	1
52=	University of Wales Swansea	1
55	Sheffield Hallam	0
56=	Anglia Polytechnic University	-2
56=	Central England	-2
56=	De Montfort	-2
56=	Derby	-2
56=	East London	-2
56=	Keele	-2
56=	Kingston	-2
56=	Leeds Metropolitan	-2
56=	Lincoln	-2
56=	Queen Mary & Westfield College London	-2
56=	Reading	-2
56=	South Bank	-2
56=	Staffordshire	-2
56=	Thames Valley	-2
70	City	-2
71	Luton	-3
72	Huddersfield	-3
73	Liverpool John Moores	-4

The risers and fallers

TOP TEN RISERS

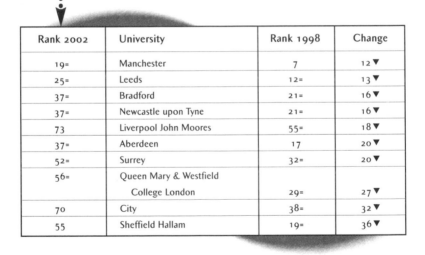

Rank 2002	University	Rank 1998	Change
37=	Westminster	62=	25 ▲
56=	De Montfort	80	24 ▲
37=	Abertay	60=	23 ▲
56=	Central England	76=	20 ▲
56=	Derby	76=	20 ▲
18	Warwick	38=	20 ▲
19=	Hull	38=	19 ▲
14	Belfast	32=	18 ▲
10=	Nottingham	27=	17 ▲
22=	Portsmouth	38=	16 ▲

'TOP' TEN FALLERS

Rank 2002	University	Rank 1998	Change
19=	Manchester	7	12 ▼
25=	Leeds	12=	13 ▼
37=	Bradford	21=	16 ▼
37=	Newcastle upon Tyne	21=	16 ▼
73	Liverpool John Moores	55=	18 ▼
37=	Aberdeen	17	20 ▼
52=	Surrey	32=	20 ▼
56=	Queen Mary & Westfield College London	29=	27 ▼
70	City	38=	32 ▼
55	Sheffield Hallam	19=	36 ▼

Once again, UMIST trounces its more celebrated colleagues to be number one. The traditional big hitters such as Imperial College London, Birmingham and Cambridge also perform well, which is perhaps to be expected, but it is their redbrick Mancunian cousin that steals the show. The former polytechnics do not seem to be doing as well here as they have done in other subjects, their leading representative being Portsmouth at 22nd equal. Sheffield Hallam loses its position as one of the three leading ex-polys by virtue of its status as the biggest faller, dropping 36 places out of the top 20 to 55th.

Of the top ten risers, De Montfort does well to drag itself up from a rock bottom 80th in 1998 to a more respectable 56th equal this year, although fewer universities are ranked, meaning it remains in the bottom 20. Warwick, Hull, Belfast and Nottingham force their way into the top 20 by climbing around 20 places each.

RANKING OF UNIVERSITIES BY VALUE-ADDED

Rank	University	Value Added (ave=0)
1	UMIST	19
2	Portsmouth	9
3=	Glamorgan	7
3=	Glasgow Caledonian	7
3=	Nottingham	7
6=	Bristol	5
6=	Sheffield Hallam	5
6=	Southampton	5
9	Hull	4
10=	Bournemouth	3
10=	Bradford	3
10=	Edinburgh	3
10=	Warwick	3
14=	Oxford Brookes	2
14=	Sheffield	2
14=	Teesside	2
17=	Exeter	1
17=	Greenwich	1
17=	Staffordshire	1
17=	West of England	1
21=	Coventry	0
21=	Luton	0

Rank	University	Value Added (ave=0)
21=	Nottingham Trent	0
24	Essex	-1
25=	Hertfordshire	-2
25=	Huddersfield	-2
25=	Liverpool	-2
25=	University of Wales Cardiff	-2
29=	Central England	-3
29=	Central Lancashire	-3
29=	De Montfort	-3
29=	East Anglia	-3
29=	Kent	-3
29=	Lancaster	-3
29=	Newcastle upon Tyne	-3
29=	Sussex	-3
29=	University of Wales Bangor	-3
29=	Westminster	-3
39=	Brighton	-4
39=	Durham	4
39=	Leeds	-4
39=	York	-4
43	Reading	-5
44	Queen Mary & Westfield College London	-9

NOTE Value-added calculations are based on the single reference course Electronic Engineering H600. Only institutions offering this course are ranked.

Despite being the biggest faller in the main ranking, Sheffield Hallam can be proud of its position in the top ten of the value-added table. Fellow ex-poly Portsmouth adds to its good performance in the main list by occupying the number two spot when it comes to value-added. But the day belongs to UMIST which, for the second subject in succession, proves its worth by claiming number one in both the points and value added rankings.

Further comments and selected quotes

UMIST's number one place in the main ranking comes as a result of stronger support from currently active recruiters in this subject area. Its advantage over former number one, London's **Imperial College**, is thus a slim one and it is quite conceivable that next year will see the two rivals swap places again.

A recruiter for a company in the Midlands avoids *'a number of non-vocationally focused ex-polytechnics'* but specifies **Portsmouth** and **Plymouth** as two of her targeted universities for electrical engineering.

One medium-sized firm from the South-East expressed a preference for **Birmingham** and **Bath**, summing up the latter in one word: *'quality'*. Despite this and other support, Bath slips ten places to 12th.

UMIST's expected A-level requirement for its highly rated Electronic Engineering course (H600) is listed in the 2001 *Big Guide* as BBC (22 points using the old UCAS points system). London's **Queen Mary & Westfield College** has the same requirements but has fallen 27 places to lie 56th equal in employers' preferences, resulting in its place at the bottom of the value-added table.

A late surge of votes in our most recent survey lifts **Strathclyde** to sixth, their highest ever ranking in this subject. This will be sure to serve them well in next year's report.

FINANCE/ACCOUNTANCY/BANKING

Employability rankings summary

Total votes: 131
Universities ranked: 53   **Not ranked:** 44
Highest: Warwick (13 points)   **Lowest:** Luton/Thames Valley (-4 points)

Recruiters' perceptions of higher education and graduates

Influence of university reputation

	Finance/Accountancy/ Banking %	All replies %
Total	0.0	0.5
Considerable	22.9	19.9
Somewhat	39.9	39.8
Slight	20.8	19.4
None	16.7	20.4

Not wanting to be different, most recruiters of finance, accountancy and banking graduates are at least slightly influenced by an institution's reputation. In fact these employers are slightly less likely to pay no heed to a graduate's university than average, since only 16.7 per cent are not influenced at all.

Changing degree standards

	Finance/Accountancy/ Banking %	All replies %
Falling	12.2	13.4
Falling slightly	32.7	39.3
No change	49.0	40.3
Rising slightly	6.1	7.0
Rising	0.0	0.0

The opinion of recruiters in this subject area appears to fall somewhere between 'no change' and 'falling slightly'. Approximately half believe that there is no change in degree standards, higher than the average, while a third think they are falling slightly. What is once again clear is that very few employers think that degrees are getting better.

New graduates' employability

	Finance/Accountancy/ Banking %	All replies %
Good	18.8	20.0
Fairly good	64.8	59.5
No view	6.3	8.8
Fairly poor	10.4	11.7
Poor	0.0	0.0

As with the general case, the vast majority of financial recruiters have a positive view of graduates when it comes to their employability. 83.6 per cent of those surveyed regard new graduates' employability as being good or fairly good.

Preferences for employability qualities

Rank	Employability qualities	Finance/Accountancy/ Banking %	All replies %
1	Enthusiasm	86.5	81.5
2	Verbal communication skills	78.8	83.8
3	Problem solving	77.8	66.9
4	Business awareness	76.9	62.5
5=	Degree classification	75.0	67.6
5=	Personal/transferable skills	75.0	66.7
7	Computing skills	71.2	59.3
8	Numeracy	69.2	64.8
9=	Teamworking	67.3	66.7
9=	Written communication skills	67.3	71.8
11	Work experience	65.4	69.9
12	A-level grades	61.5	53.7
13	Self-reliance	48.1	54.2
14	Course content	38.5	38.4
15	Sandwich course	36.5	31.5

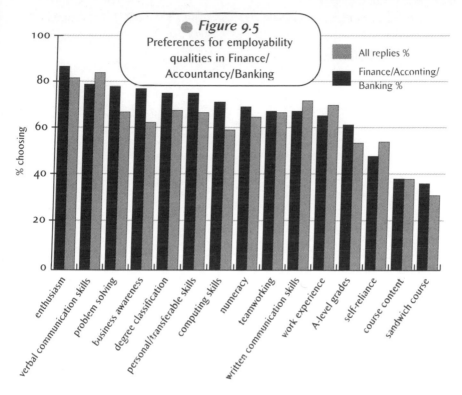

Figure 9.5
Preferences for employability qualities in Finance/Accountancy/Banking

All replies %

Finance/Acconting/Banking %

Although they exchange places here, enthusiasm and verbal communication skills remain the two most desirable qualities a graduate can have. More notably, problem solving, business awareness, numeracy and computing skills do well in comparison to the general case. It is easy to imagine that these are qualities that would be of benefit to a graduate working in the financial industry. In contrast, self-reliance is seen as less important in this subject area, which perhaps comes as a bit of a surprise.

RANKING OF UNIVERSITIES BY EMPLOYABILITY POINTS ••••

Rank	University	Employability points
1	Warwick	13
2	Manchester	12
3	London School of Economics	11
4	Bristol	10
5	Southampton	10
6	Exeter	8
7	Birmingham	7
8	Nottingham	7
9	Reading	6
10	Leeds	6
11=	Bath	5
11=	Hull	5
11=	Loughborough	5
11=	Newcastle upon Tyne	5
11=	Stirling	5
16	Oxford	5
17=	Aston	4
17=	University of Wales Bangor	4
19=	Bournemouth	3
19=	Heriot-Watt	3
19=	Sheffield	3
22	Liverpool John Moores	3
23	Cambridge	2
24=	Belfast	2
24=	Brighton	2
24=	Central England	2

Rank	University	Employability points
24=	Durham	2
24=	Essex	2
24=	Imperial College London	2
24=	Nottingham Trent	2
24=	Surrey	2
24=	Sussex	2
24=	University of Wales Aberystwyth	2
24=	University of Wales Cardiff	2
24=	University of Wales Swansea	2
36=	City	1
36=	Kings College London	1
36=	University College London	1
36=	UMIST	1
36=	Portsmouth	1
36=	York	1
42	Bradford	1
43	Leeds Metropolitan	0
44=	Lancaster	-1
44=	West of England	-1
46=	Kingston	-2
46=	London Guildhall	-2
46=	Sunderland	-2
46=	Teesside	-2
46=	Westminster	-2
51	Northumbria	-4
52=	Luton	-4
52=	Thames Valley	-4

The risers and fallers

TOP TEN RISERS

Rank 2002	University	Rank 1998	Change
24=	Central England	84=	60▲
17=	University of Wales Bangor	67=	50▲
19=	Bournemouth	67=	48▲
24=	University of Wales Aberystwyth	64=	40▲
52=	Luton	88	36▲
11=	Newcastle upon Tyne	46=	35▲
46=	Teesside	80=	34▲
24=	University of Wales Swansea	58=	34▲
24=	Brighton	56=	32▲
24=	Belfast	53=	29▲

'TOP' TEN FALLERS

Rank 2002	University	Rank 1998	Change
44=	West of England	39=	5 ▼
36=	University College London	29=	7 ▼
16	Oxford	4=	12 ▼
19=	Sheffield	7	12 ▼
19=	Heriot-Watt	3	16 ▼
36=	City	18	18 ▼
23	Cambridge	4=	19 ▼
46=	Kingston	27	19 ▼
36=	Kings College London	13=	23 ▼
36=	UMIST	10	26 ▼

As with so many subjects, the elite Russell group of universities dominates the top end of the points ranking – as they themselves would expect to do. The London School of Economics in particular will be pleased to see itself in the top three of a financial list. Some heavyweights though are dropping away somewhat: University College London, Oxford, Cambridge and Kings College London all find themselves in the 'top' ten fallers. Joining them is the biggest faller, UMIST, experiencing vastly different fortunes in this area than it has in the technical subjects.

The Welsh universities appear to be doing well with three in the top ten risers. The most successful of these is Bangor, which has benefited from a huge leap of 50 places to break away from its neighbours, who remain together at 24th equal. Meanwhile, at the bottom, it is becoming a depressingly familiar story for Luton and Thames Valley.

RANKING OF UNIVERSITIES BY VALUE-ADDED ••••

Rank	University	Value Added (ave=0)
1	Napier	8
2	Nottingham Trent	7
3=	Central England	5
3=	Lincoln	5
5=	Abertay	3
5=	Derby	3
5=	Glasgow Caledonian	3
5=	Greenwich	3
5=	London Guildhall	3
5=	Sheffield Hallam	3
5=	University of Wales Bangor	3
12=	Hull	2
12=	Portsmouth	2
12=	Stirling	2
12=	University of Wales Aberystwyth	2
16=	Central Lancashire	1
16=	Middlesex	1
16=	Staffordshire	1

Rank	University	Value Added (ave=0)
16=	Wolverhampton	1
20	Birmingham	0
21=	Aberdeen	-1
21=	Dundee	-1
21=	Essex	-1
21=	Paisley	-1
25=	Hertfordshire	-2
25=	Newcastle upon Tyne	-2
27=	Liverpool	-3
27=	Sunderland	-3
29	University of Wales Cardiff	-4
30=	Kent	-5
30=	Strathclyde	-5
30=	Ulster	-5
33	East Anglia	-6
34=	Glasgow Caledonian	-7
34=	Northumbria	-7
36=	Belfast	-8
36=	Lancaster	-8

NOTE Value-added calculations are based on the single reference course Accountancy N400. Only institutions offering this course are ranked.

Central England makes the most of its position as the biggest riser in the main ranking by securing a top three place according to value-added. Bangor also enhances its position as the leading Welsh university by just about reaching the top ten here. Central England's good position, plus Napier and Nottingham Trent's occupancy of the top two places, confirms that a so-called 'weaker' university can be just as good an option as one of the traditionally better-placed institutions.

Further comments and selected quotes

Caution: although 52 survey participants were actively recruiting in this subject area, there were relatively few votes per university. This means that a handful of votes can make a considerable difference to the rankings.

After seven years of floating about the top three, **Warwick** takes over as number one, its second in this year's subject reports. Former leader **Manchester** slips to second.

Six universities are new to the top ten compared with the 1998 standings: **Bristol**, **Southampton**, **Exeter**, **Birmingham**, **Nottingham** and **Reading**, whose climb from 34th equal just fails to warrant inclusion in the top ten risers.

The employability of **Bournemouth**'s graduates is recognised by two top 20 appearances for the first time. Bournemouth reaches these giddy heights both in business (page 54) and here, where it is now the leading former polytechnic.

The relatively modest rankings for **Oxford** and **Cambridge** are reflected by the comments of one Midlands-based accountant who observed that Oxbridge graduates *'can be over-academic'*. A London recruiter, who admitted to being considerably influenced by a university's reputation, thinks *'they produce very clever people with no common sense'* and instead prefers graduates of **Stirling**'s MSc in Fund Management, which he describes as the *'perfect employability course'*.

Thames Valley is noted as being *'particularly weak'* by one Middlesex-based accountancy practice where one partner's opinion is based on the *'graduates employed by us'*.

GENERAL/OTHER ENGINEERING

Employability rankings summary

Total votes: 395
Universities ranked: 82   **Not ranked:** 15
Highest: UMIST (47 points)   **Lowest:** De Montfort (-6 points)

Recruiters' perceptions of higher education and graduates

Influence of university reputation

	General Engineering %	All replies %
Total	2.3	0.5
Considerable	20.5	19.9
Somewhat	50.0	39.8
Slight	15.9	19.4
None	11.4	20.4

2.3 per cent of employers of general engineering graduates confess to being totally influenced by the reputation of a university in their recruitment practice. It is not a huge proportion by any means but striking because this figure tends to be zero. In keeping with this, and the results for other engineering disciplines, nearly nine out of ten recruiters indicate that they take university into account to some extent, somewhat or more when selecting new graduates.

Changing degree standards

	General Engineering %	All replies %
Falling	13.3	13.4
Falling slightly	40.0	39.3
No change	40.0	40.3
Rising slightly	6.7	7.0
Rising	0.0	0.0

General engineering recruiters have a pretty bleak view of degree standards, with more than half selecting 'falling' or 'falling slightly'. In fact the results here are almost identical to the average.

New graduates' employability

	General Engineering %	All replies %
Good	16.3	20.0
Fairly good	60.5	59.5
No view	7.0	8.8
Fairly poor	16.3	11.7
Poor	0.0	0.0

It would appear that more recruiters in this subject would regard new graduates' employability as poor than is usual. However, over three-quarters still rate it as being fairly good or good.

Preferences for employability qualities

Rank	Employability qualities	General Engineering %	All replies %
1	Degree classification	86.7	67.6
2=	Verbal communication skills	84.4	83.8
2=	Enthusiasm	84.4	81.5
4	Work experience	75.6	69.9
5	Problem solving	72.0	66.9
6=	Written communication skills	68.9	71.8
6=	Numeracy	68.9	64.8
8=	Business awareness	66.7	62.5
8=	Teamworking	66.7	66.7
8=	Personal/transferable skills	66.7	66.7
11	A-level grades	64.4	53.7
12	Self-reliance	57.8	54.2
13	Computing skills	55.6	59.3
14	Sandwich course	48.9	31.5
15	Second language	42.2	22.7

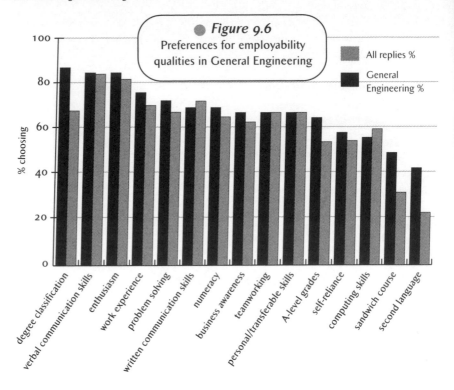

Figure 9.6
Preferences for employability qualities in General Engineering

Much like other engineering subjects, the results here indicate that recruiters of general engineering graduates place relative emphasis on degree classification, work experience, problem solving and sandwich course. This is understandable because they are the kinds of skills you would expect to be useful in an engineering career. What is more surprising is the strong showing for a second language. Maybe engineering firms have been branching out and exploring overseas markets of late.

RANKING OF UNIVERSITIES BY EMPLOYABILITY POINTS ••••

Rank	University	Employability points
1	UMIST	47
2	Loughborough	40
3	Imperial College London	33
4	Nottingham	32
5	Cambridge	27
6	Bath	26
7	Birmingham	25
8	Brunel	24
9=	Manchester	22
9=	Strathclyde	22
11	Bristol	20
12	Heriot-Watt	20
13	Sheffield	20
14	Aston	16
15	Oxford	14
16	Warwick	14
17	Edinburgh	13
18	Leeds	13
19	Southampton	11
20	Newcastle upon Tyne	11
21	Liverpool	9
22	Glasgow	8
23	Durham	8
24	Salford	8
25	Nottingham Trent	7
26=	Bradford	7
26=	Hertfordshire	7
28	Belfast	6
29=	Exeter	5
29=	Hull	5
29=	Surrey	5
29=	University of Wales Cardiff	5
29=	York	5
34=	Stirling	4
34=	University College London	4
36=	Aberdeen	4
36=	Napier	4
36=	Robert Gordon	4
39=	Lancaster	3
39=	Kings College London	3
39=	Oxford Brookes	3
39=	Paisley	3
39=	St Andrews	3
44=	Portsmouth	2
44=	Ulster	2
46=	Abertay	2
46=	Essex	2
46=	Glasgow Caledonian	2
46=	Manchester Metropolitan	2
46=	Northumbria	2
46=	Teesside	2
46=	University of Wales Swansea	2
46=	West of England	2
54	Plymouth	1
55=	Brighton	1
55=	East Anglia	1
55=	Kent	1
55=	Westminster	1
59	Kingston	1
60=	East London	-1
60=	Greenwich	-1
60=	Keele	-1
60=	Queen Mary & Westfield College London	-1
60=	Luton	-1
60=	Middlesex	-1
60=	Thames Valley	-1
67=	Coventry	-1
67=	Sheffield Hallam	-1
69=	Anglia Polytechnic University	-2
69=	Derby	-2
69=	Reading	-2
69=	Sussex	-2
69=	Wolverhampton	-2
74	Huddersfield	-2
75=	South Bank	-3
75=	Staffordshire	-3
77	City	-3
78=	Central England	-4
78=	Leeds Metropolitan	-4
78=	Lincoln	-4
78=	Liverpool John Moores	-4
82	De Montfort	-6

The risers and fallers

TOP TEN RISERS

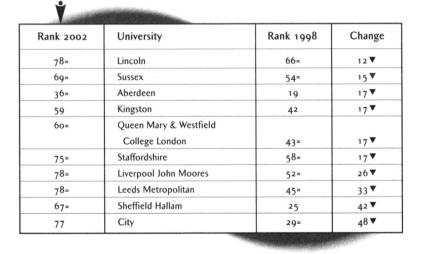

Rank 2002	University	Rank 1998	Change
29=	University of Wales Cardiff	65	36 ▲
39=	Oxford Brookes	70=	31 ▲
46	Essex	70=	24 ▲
60=	Thames Valley	83	23 ▲
34=	Stirling	54=	20 ▲
46=	West of England	66=	20 ▲
60=	Luton	79	19 ▲
39=	Paisley	58=	19 ▲
28	Belfast	45=	17 ▲
55=/69=	Westminster/Wolverhampton	70=/84	15 ▲

'TOP' TEN FALLERS

Rank 2002	University	Rank 1998	Change
78=	Lincoln	66=	12 ▼
69=	Sussex	54=	15 ▼
36=	Aberdeen	19	17 ▼
59	Kingston	42	17 ▼
60=	Queen Mary & Westfield College London	43=	17 ▼
75=	Staffordshire	58=	17 ▼
78=	Liverpool John Moores	52=	26 ▼
78=	Leeds Metropolitan	45=	33 ▼
67=	Sheffield Hallam	25	42 ▼
77	City	29=	48 ▼

UMIST continues its excellent showing in the technical subjects. It adds a top spot here to ninth in civil engineering, joint 11th in maths/statistics, second in science and two more first places in electrical engineering/electronics and computing/IT. If there is one university that proves that different institutions excel in different subjects it is UMIST.

RANKING OF UNIVERSITIES BY VALUE-ADDED

Rank	University	Value Added (ave=0)
1	Loughborough	27
2	Brunel	19
3	Heriot-Watt	11
4	Birmingham	10
5	Leeds	6
6	Cambridge	5
7=	Huddersfield	3
7=	Napier	3
9	Warwick	1
10	Edinburgh	0
11	Salford	-1
12	Liverpool	-4
13	Oxford	-7
14=	Durham	-9
14=	Portsmouth	-9
14=	Surrey	-9
17	Lancaster	-10
18=	Aberdeen	-11
18=	Leicester	-11
20	Queen Mary & Westfield College London	-12

NOTE Value-added calculations are based on the single reference course Engineering H100. Only institutions offering this course are ranked.

Eight of the top ten in the value-added list appear in the leading 20 of the general ranking. This eight includes Cambridge, suggesting that even high-achieving students can substantially improve themselves at university. Loughborough's value-added is spectacularly high and coupled with its second position in the main list makes this university *the* standout institution in this subject, as it is in civil engineering.

Bottom position in the value-added table goes to Queen Mary & Westfield. The London college is also one of the big fallers and takes up a lowly position in the main ranking – quite a disappointing year.

Further comments and selected quotes

This is the fifth successive year that UMIST is the employers' number one for general engineering. Over the same period Loughborough has risen from seventh to second. A large southern-based recruiter, who is considerably influenced by her perception of a university, speaks of UMIST's *'high quality engineering graduates'*. A Midlands company, where influence is described as 'somewhat', refers specifically to the *'good reputation of chemical engineering'* at Loughborough.

One survey participant admitting to being considerably influenced by university reputation explicitly cites Sheffield Hallam as being *'particularly avoided'*. Perhaps as a result they fall from 25th in 1998 to 67th equal now, a decline only exceeded by the 48 places experienced by City.

If rankings were based on the most recent survey only, UMIST and Loughborough would still fill the top two places, but Nottingham would lie third. These recent votes could enhance their standing in future results.

A small, East of England firm praises Hertfordshire from their experience of a *'recent graduate recruited'*, while a Northern company base their support for the same university on its *'sandwich links'* and *'good academic liaison'*. Hertfordshire remains one of the

preferred former polytechnics but is still narrowly out-scored by **Nottingham Trent**, leaders in the subject since 1999.

One Scottish recruiter's preference for graduates from **Strathclyde** is based on its *'good standard of teaching'*. Strathclyde's popularity is not just restricted to local firms though. A medium-sized company in the South of England singles it, and Scottish universities in general, out for praise because of the *'maturity of their graduates'*.

LANGUAGES

Employability rankings summary

Total votes: 155
Universities ranked: 97   **Not ranked:** 0
Highest: Cambridge (10 points)   **Lowest:** Derby (-4 points)

Recruiters' perceptions of higher education and graduates

Influence of university reputation

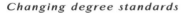

	Languages %	All replies %
Total	0.0	0.5
Considerable	26.1	19.9
Somewhat	34.8	39.8
Slight	26.1	19.4
None	13.0	20.4

In what is now a familiar scenario, we can see that employers of languages graduates appear to select their new recruits with their university or college firmly in mind. In fact, a *smaller* proportion of recruiters claim *not* to be influenced at all than for all subjects put together – only 13 per cent in this subject compared with 20.4 per cent on average.

Changing degree standards

	Languages %	All replies %
Falling	4.3	13.4
Falling slightly	43.5	39.3
No change	47.8	40.3
Rising slightly	4.3	7.0
Rising	0.0	0.0

Here, recruiters seem to have a slightly brighter outlook than average. In contrast with most other subjects, the majority of languages recruiters think that degree standards are *not*

falling. However, it is a slim majority as almost 50 per cent believe standards are 'falling slightly' at least.

New graduates' employability

	Languages %	All replies %
Good	42.9	20.0
Fairly good	42.9	59.5
No view	4.8	8.8
Fairly poor	9.5	11.7
Poor	0.0	0.0

In a similar vein, recruiters in this subject hold graduates in even higher regard than most. Almost 90 per cent think that the graduates they employ are either good or fairly good. Furthermore, 42.9 per cent choosing 'good' is more than double the average.

Preferences for employability qualities

Rank	Employability qualities	Languages %	All replies %
1	Teamworking	87.0	66.7
2=	Personal/transferable skills	82.6	66.7
2=	Enthusiasm	82.6	81.5
4	Verbal communication skills	78.3	83.8
5	Business awareness	73.9	62.5
6	Degree classification	69.6	67.6
7=	Computing skills	65.2	59.3
7=	Work experience	65.2	69.9
9	Numeracy	60.9	64.8
10	Problem solving	60.0	66.9
11	A-level grades	56.5	53.7
12=	Second language	52.2	22.7
12=	Self-reliance	52.2	54.2
14	Written communication skills	47.8	71.8
15	Course content	43.5	38.4

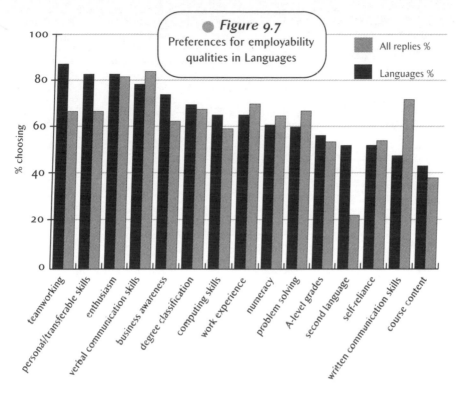

● Figure 9.7
Preferences for employability qualities in Languages

All replies %

Languages %

It is strange that for a subject area where communication is key, those skills are seen as relatively less important. Perhaps employers are assuming that languages graduates will have developed good verbal and written communication skills anyway and are thus less inclined to specify them in a survey. Similarly, despite being far more significant than average, having a second language is perhaps not as high up the list as we would expect.

The other qualities that stand out – teamworking, personal/transferable skills and business awareness – are similar to those that were prominent in the results for business. This probably reflects the fact that careers using languages cover a wide variety of fields, the world of business in particular.

RANKING OF UNIVERSITIES BY EMPLOYABILITY POINTS ••••

Rank	University	Employability points
1	Cambridge	10
2	Oxford	9
3	Edinburgh	8
4	Durham	8
5=	Exeter	7
5=	Leeds	7
5=	Nottingham	7
8	St Andrews	6
9	Bath	5
10=	Aston	4
10=	Bradford	4
10=	Lancaster	4
10=	Plymouth	4
10=	Sheffield	4
10=	Warwick	4
16=	Birmingham	3
16=	Bournemouth	3
16=	Bristol	3
16=	East Anglia	3
16=	Glasgow	3
16=	Hull	3
16=	London School of Economics	3
16=	University College London	3
16=	Manchester	3
16=	Reading	3
16=	Stirling	3
27=	Aberdeen	2
27=	Belfast	2
27=	Brunel	2
27=	City	2
27=	De Montfort	2
27=	Dundee	2
27=	Heriot-Watt	2
27=	Huddersfield	2
27=	Keele	2
27=	Leicester	2
27=	Goldsmiths College London	2
27=	Imperial College London	2
27=	Kings College London	2
27=	Queen Mary & Westfield College London	2
27=	Royal Holloway London	2
27=	London Guildhall	2
27=	Loughborough	2
27=	Nottingham Trent	2
27=	Oxford Brookes	2
27=	Portsmouth	2
27=	Salford	2
27=	Sheffield Hallam	2
27=	Strathclyde	2
27=	Ulster	2

Rank	University	Employability points
27=	University of Wales Bangor	2
27=	University of Wales Cardiff	2
27=	University of Wales Swansea	2
27=	Westminster	2
27=	West of England	2
56	Liverpool	1
57	Northumbria	0
58=	Brighton	-1
58=	Central Lancashire	-1
58=	Kent	-1
58=	Sussex	-1
58=	York	-1
63=	Abertay	-2
63=	Anglia Polytechnic University	-2
63=	Buckingham	-2
63=	Central England	-2
63=	Coventry	-2
63=	East London	-2
63=	Essex	-2
63=	Glamorgan	-2
63=	Glasgow Caledonian	-2
63=	Greenwich	-2
63=	Hertfordshire	-2
63=	Kingston	-2
63=	Leeds Metropolitan	-2
63=	Lincoln	-2
63=	Liverpool John Moores	-2
63=	UMIST	-2
63=	Manchester Metropolitan	-2
63=	Middlesex	-2
63=	Napier	-2
63=	Newcastle upon Tyne	-2
63=	North London	-2
63=	Paisley	-2
63=	Robert Gordon	-2
63=	Southampton	-2
63=	South Bank	-2
63=	Staffordshire	-2
63=	Sunderland	-2
63=	Surrey	-2
63=	Teesside	-2
63=	University of Wales Aberystwyth	-2
63=	University of Wales Lampeter	-2
63=	Wolverhampton	-2
95=	Luton	-3
95=	Thames Valley	-3
97	Derby	-4

The risers and fallers

TOP TEN RISERS

Rank 2002	University	Rank 1998	Change
16=	Glasgow	35=	19▲
16=	University College London	35=	19▲
16=	Stirling	35=	19▲
27=	De Montfort	42=	15▲
10=	Bradford	23=	13▲
10=	Sheffield	23=	13▲
27=	Heriot-Watt	35=	8▲
27=	Royal Holloway London	35=	8▲
16=	London School of Economics	23=	7▲
5=	Nottingham	12=	7▲

'TOP' TEN FALLERS

Rank 2002	University	Rank 1998	Change
56	Liverpool	23=	33▼
58=	Sussex	23=	35▼
63=	Coventry	23=	40▼
58=	Kent	18=	40▼
63=	Newcastle upon Tyne	23=	40▼
63=	University of Wales Aberystwyth	23=	40▼
58=	York	18=	40▼
63=	Southampton	12=	51▼
95=	Thames Valley	41	54▼
97	Derby	42=	55▼

For the first of three times in this year's survey, Oxford and Cambridge live up to their billing by sharing the top two positions. They are joined in the top ten by a selection of other prestigious old institutions, although the leading former polytechnic, Plymouth, is knocking on the door at tenth equal.

The list of the top ten risers is peppered with institutions from Scotland and London. Of those travelling in the opposite direction, Kent, York and Southampton suffer the biggest falls from grace, dropping, as they do, well out of the top 20.

RANKING OF UNIVERSITIES BY VALUE-ADDED

Rank	University	Value Added (ave=o)
1	Oxford Brookes	13
2	Northumbria	6
3=	North London	4
3=	Bradford	4
3=	Wolverhampton	4
6=	Stirling	3
6=	Leeds	3
8=	Kingston	2
8=	Edinburgh	2
8=	Aberdeen	2
8=	Queen Mary & Westfield College London	2
8=	Warwick	2
8=	Lancaster	2
14=	Nottingham	1
14=	Aston	1
14=	Hull	1
14=	Leicester	1

Rank	University	Value Added (ave=o)
14=	Bath	1
14=	East Anglia	1
14=	Luton	1
21=	Sheffield	0
21=	St Andrews	0
21=	Belfast	0
24=	Birmingham	-1
24=	Glasgow	-1
24=	Reading	-1
24=	Bristol	-1
28=	University College London	-2
28=	University of Wales Cardiff	-2
28=	Kings College London	-2
28=	University of Wales Aberystwyth	-2
32	Liverpool	-3
33	Royal Holloway London	-4
34	Newcastle	-5
35	Southampton	-8
36	Kent	-9

NOTE Value-added calculations are based on the single reference course French R100. Only institutions offering this course are ranked.

Oxford Brookes has produced a storming performance in this subject in the value-added stakes. After reaching a respectable 27th equal in the main list, the former polytechnic tops the value-added ranking by quite a margin. Joining it in the top ten are, among others, North London, Wolverhampton and Kingston, belying their lowly positions in the main table.

Further comments and selected quotes

Birmingham, Bristol and Manchester all relinquish their top ten status. This is partially due to the low 'turnout' in this subject, as is the substantial falls of over 50 places by Derby and Thames Valley. Southampton's similar fall takes them from 12th equal to 63rd equal.

High entry requirements coupled with few compliments from survey participants results in three London institutions – Kings College, University College and Royal Holloway – appearing among the ten universities with the lowest value-added.

Caution: The scale of graduate recruitment is lower in languages than in any other subject area surveyed. This means that a handful of votes can make a considerable difference to the rankings. Even so, a third successive year as the employers' favourites is an impressive achievement for Cambridge.

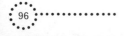

LAW

Employability rankings summary

Total votes: 103
Universities ranked: 48   **Not ranked:** 49
Highest: Oxford (12 points)   **Lowest:** Lincoln/Sheffield Hallam (-2 points)

Recruiters' perceptions of higher education and graduates

Influence of university reputation

	Law %	All replies %
Total	0.0	0.5
Considerable	33.3	19.9
Somewhat	55.5	39.8
Slight	0.0	19.4
None	11.1	20.4

It appears that a law graduate's university or college is a major factor in employers' recruitment decisions. Almost 90 per cent responded that they were either somewhat or considerably influenced in their thinking by an institution's reputation. This is perhaps to be expected in an old school profession like law above other subject areas.

Changing degree standards

	Law %	All replies %
Falling	0.0	13.4
Falling slightly	30.0	39.3
No change	70.0	40.3
Rising slightly	0.0	7.0
Rising	0.0	0.0

Although the small size of the sample (see 'Further comments and selected quotes') could be coming into play here (and throughout this subject) it looks as if recruiters of law graduates are more clear-cut in their feeling towards the standards of contemporary higher education. With 70 per cent opting for 'no change' it would seem that they have a fairly neutral view of degree standards, erring slightly on the side of 'falling'.

New graduates' employability

	Law %	All replies %
Good	66.7	20.0
Fairly good	33.3	59.5
No view	0.0	8.8
Fairly poor	0.0	11.7
Poor	0.0	0.0

In keeping with the relatively positive tone of the *Changing Degree Standards* table, the results here reveal a unanimous vote of confidence for law graduates. 100 per cent of employers regard their new recruits as exhibiting at least fairly good employability. Once again, this clear-cut result probably has something to do with the small sample size, but it is not inconceivable to think that law graduates as a group are of an inherently employable character.

Preferences for employability qualities

Rank	Employability qualities	Law %	All replies %
1	A-level grades	100.0	53.7
2=	Computing skills	80.0	59.3
2=	Degree classification	80.0	67.6
4=	Business awareness	70.0	62.5
4=	Teamworking	70.0	66.7
4=	Verbal communication skills	70.0	83.8
4=	Self-reliance	70.0	54.2
8=	Work experience	60.0	69.9
8=	Written communication skills	60.0	71.8
8=	Enthusiasm	60.0	81.5
11=	Sports & hobbies	50.0	27.3
11=	Personal/transferable skills	50.0	66.7
11=	Numeracy	50.0	64.8
11=	Problem solving	50.0	66.9
15	Course content	40.0	38.4

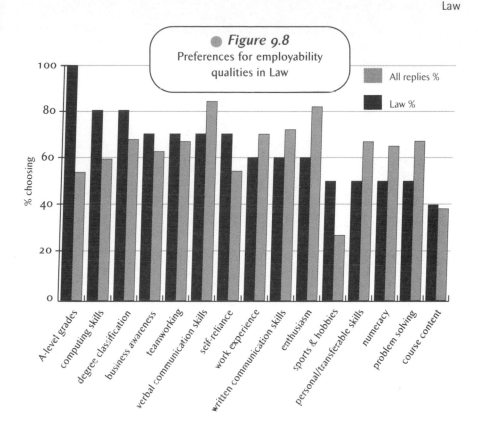

Figure 9.8
Preferences for employability qualities in Law

All replies %
Law %

In almost every respect, the subject-specific results displayed here are very different from the general case. In particular, the two qualities that shine in more subjects than not – verbal communication skills and enthusiasm – are not anywhere near as high up the list for law. This is particularly surprising for the former, the common image of a lawyer being one of an individual verbally arguing his or her case. Just as surprising, and perhaps more inexplicable, is the good performance of computing skills which sits alongside A-level grades and degree classification in the top three. It is easier to accept the presence here of the latter two qualities as they are clear evidence of a graduate's ability to apply themselves to involving material and achieve the required results, often under no small amount of pressure. Having said this, 100 per cent support for A-level grades is doubtless in part a statistical blip.

RANKING OF UNIVERSITIES •••• BY EMPLOYABILITY POINTS

Rank	University	Employability points
1	Oxford	12
2	Cambridge	11
3=	London School of Economics	8
3=	Southampton	8
5=	Bristol	7
5=	Kings College London	7
5=	Warwick	7
8	Manchester	6
9=	Durham	6
9=	Exeter	6
9=	Queen Mary & Westfield College London	6
12	University of Wales Cardiff	5
13=	Birmingham	4
13=	East Anglia	4
13=	Hull	4
13=	Leicester	4
13=	Imperial College London	4
13=	University College London	4
13=	Nottingham	4
13=	Reading	4
13=	St Andrews	4
13=	Sheffield	4
13=	West of England	4

Rank	University	Employability points
13=	York	4
25=	Loughborough	3
25=	Newcastle upon Tyne	3
25=	University of Wales Aberystwyth	3
28=	Aberdeen	2
28=	Belfast	2
28=	Glamorgan	2
28=	Huddersfield	2
28=	Lancaster	2
28=	Leeds	2
28=	Liverpool	2
28=	Goldsmiths College London	2
28=	London Guildhall	2
28=	Northumbria	2
28=	Nottingham Trent	2
28=	Sussex	2
28=	University of Wales Swansea	2
41=	Edinburgh	1
41=	Glasgow	1
41=	Glasgow Caledonian	1
44=	Luton	-1
44=	Thames Valley	-1
46	De Montfort	-1
47=	Lincoln	-2
47=	Sheffield Hallam	-2

The risers and fallers

TOP TEN RISERS
:

Rank 2002	University	Rank 1998	Change
9=	Queen Mary & Westfield College London	35=	26 ▲
5=	Kings College London	24	19 ▲
12	University of Wales Cardiff	25=	13 ▲
13=	East Anglia	25=	12 ▲
28=	Huddersfield	40=	12 ▲
28=	London Guildhall	40=	12 ▲
13=	Reading	25=	12 ▲
3=	London School of Economics	13	10 ▲
3=	Southampton	12	9 ▲
13=	Leicester/West of England/York	20=	7 ▲

'TOP' TEN FALLERS

Rank 2002	University	Rank 1998	Change
9=/8	Exeter/Manchester	6/5	3 ▼
28=	Liverpool/Northumbria	25=	3 ▼
13=	Nottingham	8=	5 ▼
44=	Thames Valley	39=	5 ▼
13=	Birmingham	7	6 ▼
28=	Nottingham Trent	20	8 ▼
28=	Aberdeen	17=	11 ▼
28=	Leeds	16	12 ▼
41=	Glasgow	17=	24 ▼
41=	Edinburgh	3	38 ▼

It is no surprise to see Oxford and Cambridge, two universities with a great tradition of teaching law, sitting on top of our main ranking. The remainder of the top ten is similarly dominated by the old guard. Queen Mary & Westfield College's appearance at ninth equal – and top of the risers list – is a welcome boost for an institution that has performed disappointingly in other subjects this year. At the other end it is another poor showing by the likes of Thames Valley, Luton and Sheffield Hallam (the first two of these three, however, experience much better fortunes in the value-added table below).

In addition to Queen Mary's exploits, a number of other London institutions burst into the top ten by virtue of their places in the top ten risers – Kings College, London Guildhall and the London School of Economics can all feel very pleased with themselves.

RANKING OF UNIVERSITIES BY VALUE-ADDED

Rank	University	Value Added (ave=0)
1	Thames Valley	11
2=	Anglia Polytechnic University	6
2=	Teesside	6
4=	Glamorgan	4
4=	Huddersfield	4
4=	Oxford	4
7=	Derby	3
7=	Luton	3
9=	Buckingham	2
9=	Central England	2
9=	Central Lancashire	2
9=	East London	2
9=	Greenwich	2
9=	Queen Mary & Westfield College London	2
9=	London Guildhall	2
9=	Middlesex	2
9=	Napier	2
9=	North London	2
9=	Southampton	2
9=	South Bank	2
9=	Staffordshire	2
9=	Sunderland	2
9=	Wolverhampton	2
24=	Cambridge	1
24=	Hertfordshire	1
24=	London School of Economics	1
24=	University of Wales Aberystwyth	1
24=	West of England	1
29=	Bristol	0
29=	Exeter	0
29=	Hull	0
29=	Lincoln	0
29=	Kings College London	0

Rank	University	Value Added (ave=0)
29=	Nottingham Trent University	0
29=	Plymouth	0
36=	Reading	-1
36=	University of Wales Cardiff	-1
36=	Warwick	-1
39=	Dundee	-2
39=	Durham	-2
39=	East Anglia	-2
39=	Leeds Metropolitan	-2
39=	Leicester	-2
39=	Liverpool John Moores	-2
39=	Manchester	-2
39=	Manchester Metropolitan	-2
39=	Sheffield Hallam	-2
39=	University of Wales Swansea	-2
39=	Westminster	-2
50=	De Montfort	-3
50=	Newcastle upon Tyne	-3
52=	Belfast	-4
52=	Birmingham	-4
52=	Brunel	-4
52=	City	-4
52=	Keele	-4
52=	Kingston	-4
52=	Northumbria	-4
52=	Nottingham	-4
52=	Sheffield	-4
52=	Sussex	-4
62	University College London	-5
63=	Essex	-6
63=	Kent	-6
63=	Leeds	-6
63=	Liverpool	-6
63=	Oxford Brookes	-6

NOTE Value-added calculations are based on the single reference course Law M300. Only institutions offering this course are ranked.

Apparently laughing in the face of its position in the bottom ten of the main list, Thames Valley pops up at the top of the value-added ranking, providing further evidence for the argument that not all universities are as they initially seem. Luton does almost as well but other poor performers in the points table, De Montfort and Sheffield Hallam, fail to claw back as much credit here, appearing at 39th equal and 50th equal respectively.

Further comments and selected quotes

In eight years of these reports, the **Oxbridge** institutions have shared the first two places in the law rankings. After two years of joint leadership, employers now rate **Oxford** as number one on its own.

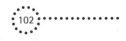

One London recruiter cast votes for each of the well-ranked **London** colleges. Her strongest preference, however, is for **Southampton** and **West of England**'s *'graduates of uniformly high quality'*.

In an earlier survey, another London firm, recruiting around 80 graduates this year, offered strong praise for the *'very few applicants, but of a very high standard'* they see from **East Anglia**. 13th for law is their highest ranking for any subject.

As mentioned on a couple of occasions, **Thames Valley** and **Luton** do not often appear near the top of university league tables. Neither received any positive votes but still perform no worse than many more celebrated departments and better than might be predicted from their modest entry requirements (for Law M300). Hence their good positions in the value-added table.

One anonymous participant helps to lift *'particularly good'* **Warwick** to fifth place, while their identification of **De Montfort** as *'weak'* is one of the reasons it falls to 46th.

Caution: The scale of graduate recruitment is low relative to other areas surveyed. This means relatively few active recruiters, votes, opinions and providers, and that a handful of votes can make a considerable difference to the results.

MATHEMATICS/STATISTICS

Employability rankings summary

Total votes: 149
Universities ranked: 54
Highest: Cambridge (24 points)

Not ranked: 43
Lowest: Aston/Manchester Metropolitan/Reading (-2 points)

Recruiters' perceptions of higher education and graduates

Influence of university reputation

	Maths/Statistics %	All replies %
Total	2.6	0.5
Considerable	17.9	19.9
Somewhat	35.9	39.8
Slight	20.5	19.4
None	23.1	20.4

Almost 3 per cent of recruiters of maths and statistics graduates own up to being totally influenced by the reputation of universities and colleges – by no means a large proportion but still unusually high. However, at the other end of the scale, slightly more maths/statistics recruiters than average experience no such influence whatsoever. On balance, the majority take a graduate's institution into account at least slightly.

Changing degree standards

	Maths/Statistics %	All replies %
Falling	9.8	13.4
Falling slightly	39.0	39.3
No change	46.3	40.3
Rising slightly	4.9	7.0
Rising	0.0	0.0

It is refreshing that the majority of recruiters in this subject do not think that degree standards are falling. But before mathematics and statistics students start breaking out the champagne, it should be noted that this majority is so small it is hardly worthy of the name and nearly half of employers still think standards are getting poorer.

New graduates' employability

	Maths/Statistics %	All replies %
Good	17.1	20.0
Fairly good	61.0	59.5
No view	12.2	8.8
Fairly poor	9.8	11.7
Poor	0.0	0.0

Although ever such a slightly smaller proportion of maths/statistics recruiters than average think new graduates' employability is fairly good or good, slightly fewer believe it is fairly poor. The good news, as with all subjects, is that most have a positive view of their new recruits.

Preferences for employability qualities

Rank	Employability qualities	Maths/Statistics %	All replies %
1=	A-level grades	76.2	53.7
1=	Verbal communication skills	76.2	83.8
3=	Degree classification	73.8	67.6
3=	Enthusiasm	73.8	81.5
5=	Computing skills	71.4	59.3
5=	Numeracy	71.4	64.8
7	Problem solving	70.0	66.9
8	Personal/transferable skills	69.0	66.7
9	Written communication skills	66.7	71.8
10=	Business awareness	64.3	62.5
10=	Work experience	64.3	69.9
12	Teamworking	61.9	66.7
13	Self-reliance	47.6	54.2
14	Sandwich course	42.9	31.5
15	Course content	40.5	38.4

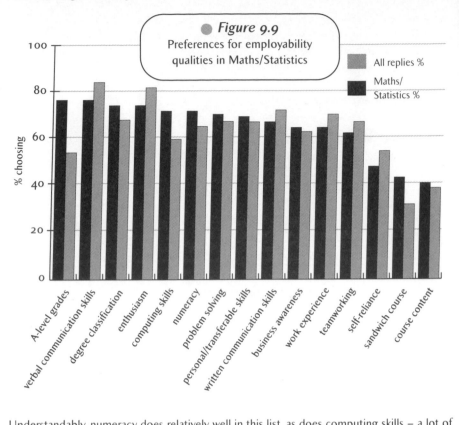

● *Figure 9.9*
Preferences for employability qualities in Maths/Statistics

Understandably, numeracy does relatively well in this list, as does computing skills – a lot of mathematics graduates go on to careers in IT-related areas. Less predictable is the claiming of the top spot by A-level results – perhaps mathematics and statistics recruiters, whose businesses tend to be based on precise results, like to see tangible measures of ability in their potential employees.

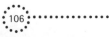

RANKING OF UNIVERSITIES BY EMPLOYABILITY POINTS

Rank	University	Employability points
1	Cambridge	24
2	Oxford	18
3	Durham	14
4	Warwick	13
5	Nottingham	11
6	Newcastle upon Tyne	7
7	Southampton	6
8=	Manchester	6
8=	Sheffield	6
8=	York	6
11=	Glasgow	6
11=	UMIST	6
13=	Leeds	5
13=	St Andrews	5
15	Bristol	4
16=	Brunel	4
16=	Liverpool John Moores	4
16=	Imperial College London	4
16=	Queen Mary & Westfield College London	4
20	Stirling	3
21	Birmingham	3
22=	Exeter	3
22=	University College London	3
22=	Surrey	3
25=	Aberdeen	2
25=	Bradford	2

Rank	University	Employability points
25=	Edinburgh	2
25=	Greenwich	2
25=	Heriot-Watt	2
25=	Hertfordshire	2
25=	Kent	2
25=	Leeds Metropolitan	2
25=	Napier	2
25=	Nottingham Trent	2
25=	Oxford Brookes	2
25=	Plymouth	2
25=	Sheffield Hallam	2
25=	Strathclyde	2
25=	University of Wales Cardiff	2
25=	University of Wales Swansea	2
41=	Bath	1
41=	Belfast	1
41=	Kings College London	1
44=	De Montfort	1
44=	Thames Valley	1
46	London School of Economics	0
47=	Lancaster	0
47=	Westminster	0
49	Ulster	-1
50=	Central England	-1
50=	Luton	-1
52=	Aston	-2
52=	Manchester Metropolitan	-2
52=	Reading	-2

The risers and fallers

Mathematics/statistics were not included in the 1998 survey so there are no comparative results to create a list of risers and fallers.

The good news for budding mathematics and statistics students is that there are very few negative scores in the points table, suggesting that most universities are doing the right things in this subject. At the top of the pile come both Oxford and Cambridge, for the third and final time in this year's survey. UMIST, putting in its usual strong performance in the technical subjects, joins them in the top 15.

RANKING OF UNIVERSITIES BY VALUE-ADDED

Rank	University	Value Added (ave=0)
1	Cambridge	12
2=	Goldsmiths College London	9
2=	North London	9
4=	Glamorgan	7
4=	Heriot-Watt	7
4=	Oxford	7
7	Durham	6
8=	Northumbria	5
8=	Sheffield Hallam	5
8=	Westminster	5
11=	Plymouth	4
11=	Stirling	4
13=	Aberdeen	3
13=	Central Lancashire	3
13=	Dundee	3
13=	Glasgow	3
13=	Kingston	3
13=	Manchester Metropolitan	3
13=	Nottingham Trent	3
20=	Hertfordshire	2
20=	Newcastle upon Tyne	2
22=	Brighton	1
22=	Warwick	1
24=	Brunel	0
24=	UMIST	0
24=	Nottingham	0
27=	City	-1
27=	Coventry	-1
27=	Hull	-1
27=	Keele	-1
27=	Queen Mary & Westfield College London	-1

Rank	University	Value Added (ave=0)
27=	Manchester	-1
27=	Sheffield	-1
27=	Southampton	-1
27=	University of Wales Aberystwyth	-1
27=	University of Wales Bangor	-1
37=	Belfast	-2
37=	Birmingham	-2
37=	Exeter	-2
37=	Leeds	-2
37=	St Andrews	-2
37=	York	-2
43=	Edinburgh	-3
43=	Essex	-3
43=	Kent	-3
43=	Leicester	-3
43=	Portsmouth	-3
43=	Sussex	-3
43=	University of Wales Cardiff	-3
50=	East Anglia	-5
50=	Lancaster	-5
50=	Liverpool	-5
50=	Loughborough	-5
50=	Reading	-5
50=	Strathclyde	-5
56	Bath	-6
57=	Bristol	-7
57=	Imperial College London	-7
57=	Royal Holloway London	-7
60=	Kings College London	-8
60=	University College London	-8

NOTE Value-added calculations are based on the single reference course Mathematics G100. Only institutions offering this course are ranked.

Despite its stringent entry requirements, Cambridge uses its impressive haul of employability points to top the value-added table. Oxford and Durham also do well and are not far behind. It appears that students with more modest A-level achievements can nevertheless obtain a good reputation with employers by attending such institutions as Heriot-Watt, Sheffield Hallam, Westminster, Plymouth and Stirling, all of which take a place in the top 15.

Further comments and selected quotes

Cambridge is the clear number one with employers. **Oxford** stays second to maintain the Oxbridge domination that has been apparent for the three years this subject has been included in the surveys. As mentioned, there are no comparable figures for 1998 from which universities' change in status can be derived.

Liverpool John Moores remains as the leading former polytechnic on the strength of the support it received in the 1999 survey.

Though in a minority of 41 per cent, the survey's *largest* recruiter of maths graduates, a public organisation in London, cites *'course content'* as an important factor in recruitment.

A Northern recruiter stresses the importance of graduates possessing business awareness – specified by 64 per cent overall. She confirms her vote for **Sheffield** because its graduates are *'commercially aware'.* **York** also receives local support from an accountancy firm because of their experience of *'successful graduate recruitment'.* A third Northern firm particularly likes the *'calibre of previous recruits over the last four years'* from **Newcastle**.

Caution: Despite 42 active recruiters and more than 1,500 recruits, voting is heavily concentrated on a few universities, leaving 43 unranked. Of the 54 that are ranked, one extra vote either way can make a big difference to an institution's rank.

SCIENCE

Employability rankings summary

Total votes: 162
Universities ranked: 58   **Not ranked:** 39
Highest: Cambridge (21 points)   **Lowest:** South Bank (-2 points)

Recruiters' perceptions of higher education and graduates

Influence of university reputation

	Science %	All replies %
Total	2.3	0.5
Considerable	14.0	19.9
Somewhat	48.8	39.8
Slight	16.3	19.4
None	18.6	20.4

As with so many of the scientific and technical subjects, the reputation of a graduate's university or college seems to be slightly more important to a potential employer when it comes to the sciences. 65.1 per cent of science recruiters indicate that they are at least somewhat influenced by an institution's reputation, including 2.3 per cent who confess to being totally so.

Changing degree standards

	Science %	All replies %
Falling	4.4	13.4
Falling slightly	55.6	39.3
No change	33.3	40.3
Rising slightly	6.7	7.0
Rising	0.0	0.0

Unfortunately for any future scientists, a larger proportion of recruiters than average (60 per cent compared with 52.7 per cent) believe that degree standards are falling in this subject area. The silver lining to this cloud is that most think they are falling only slightly.

New graduates' employability

	Science %	All replies %
Good	26.1	20.0
Fairly good	58.7	59.5
No view	6.5	8.8
Fairly poor	8.7	11.7
Poor	0.0	0.0

As we have seen, in general, employers have a good opinion of new graduates' employability. In this case it appears to be even more positive, with the vast majority (84.8 per cent) rating their new recruits good or fairly good. And less than a tenth (8.7 per cent) thought they were fairly poor.

Preferences for employability qualities

Rank	Employability qualities	Science %	All replies %
1	Verbal communication skills	83.0	83.8
2	Enthusiasm	78.7	81.5
3	Problem solving	70.8	66.9
4=	Personal/transferable skills	70.2	66.7
4=	Work experience	70.2	69.9
6	Degree classification	68.1	67.6
7	Business awareness	66.0	62.5
8=	Teamworking	66.0	66.7
8=	Written communication skills	66.0	71.8
10	Numeracy	61.7	64.8
11	A-level grades	59.6	53.7
12	Computing skills	57.4	59.3
13	Self-reliance	53.2	54.2
14	Sandwich course	51.1	31.5
15	Course content	42.6	38.4

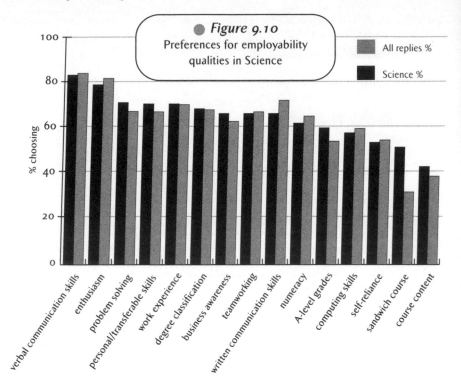

● *Figure 9.10*
Preferences for employability qualities in Science

In this respect, the results for science are very similar to the general case. Verbal communication skills and enthusiasm take up familiar positions in the top two places with 83 and 78.7 per cent support respectively. It is not much of a surprise to see problem solving move up a few places in the ranking – after all, science is all about finding answers. The one quality that exhibits a big breakaway from the average is sandwich course, which could well be down to a desire among employers to recruit scientists with a working knowledge of science in a corporate/industrial environment.

RANKING OF UNIVERSITIES BY EMPLOYABILITY POINTS

Rank	University	Employability points
1	Cambridge	21
2	UMIST	16
3	Manchester	15
4	Imperial College London	12
5	Nottingham	11
6=	Oxford	10
6=	Strathclyde	10
8	Birmingham	8
9	Sheffield	8
10=	Bristol	7
10=	Glasgow	7
10=	Heriot-Watt	7
10=	Leeds	7
14=	Edinburgh	6
14=	York	6
16=	Brunel	6
16=	Hull	6
16=	Loughborough	6
19=	University College London	5
19=	St Andrews	5
19=	Southampton	5
22	Surrey	5
23=	Leicester	4
23=	Liverpool	4
23=	Queen Mary & Westfield College London	4
23=	Newcastle upon Tyne	4
23=	Plymouth	4
23=	Reading	4

Rank	University	Employability points
23=	Salford	4
30=	Bath	3
30=	Durham	3
30=	Keele	3
30=	Kings College London	3
34	Portsmouth	2
35=	Aberdeen	2
35=	Aston	2
35=	Bradford	2
35=	De Montfort	2
35=	Hertfordshire	2
35=	Kingston	2
35=	London Guildhall	2
35=	Napier	2
35=	Paisley	2
35=	Robert Gordon	2
35=	University of Wales Aberystwyth	2
46	Sheffield Hallam	2
47=	Belfast	1
47=	Stirling	1
47=	Ulster	1
47=	Warwick	1
47=	Westminster	1
52=	Luton	-1
52=	Thames Valley	-1
54=	Anglia Polytechnic University	-2
54=	Central England	-2
54=	Derby	-2
54=	Manchester Metropolitan	-2
54=	South Bank	-2

The risers and fallers

TOP TEN RISERS

Rank 2002	University	Rank 1998	Change
35=	De Montfort	83	48 ▲
54=	Derby	89	35 ▲
35=	London Guildhall	68=	33 ▲
52=	Luton	85=	33 ▲
35=	Paisley	68=	33 ▲
52=	Thames Valley	84	32 ▲
54=	Central England	85=	31 ▲
54=	South Bank	85=	31 ▲
34	Portsmouth	61=	27 ▲
35=	Hertfordshire/Kingston	61=	26 ▲

'TOP' TEN FALLERS

Rank 2002	University	Rank 1998	Change
14=	Edinburgh	7	7 ▼
30=	Kings College London	23=	7 ▼
23=	Reading	16	7 ▼
19=	Southampton	10=	9 ▼
23=	Newcastle upon Tyne	9	14 ▼
30=	Durham	15	15 ▼
30=	Bath	14	16 ▼
46	Sheffield Hallam	28	18 ▼
54=	Manchester Metropolitan	33=	21 ▼
47=	Warwick	17=	30 ▼

It is not unusual to see UMIST ranking highly in a scientific subject, nor is it a surprise for it to be in the company of the likes of Cambridge, Manchester, Imperial, Nottingham, Oxford, Birmingham etc. Five of their research-led Russell Group peers, however, find themselves in the list of big fallers, three of which – Edinburgh, Southampton and Newcastle upon Tyne – lose their top ten status in the process. Meanwhile, Plymouth, for the second time this year, is the leading former polytechnic (the other subject being languages).

While there are some impressive moves up the table – notably, De Montfort's rise of 48 places to 35th equal – none of the top ten risers manages to break into the top 30, let alone the top ten.

RANKING OF UNIVERSITIES BY VALUE-ADDED

Rank	University	Value Added (ave=o)
1	UMIST	11
2=	Heriot-Watt	8
2=	Manchester	8
4=	De Montfort	7
4=	Paisley	7
6=	Liverpool John Moores	5
6=	North London	5
8	Kingston	4
9	Edinburgh	3
10=	Nottingham	2
10=	Salford	2
12=	Anglia Polytechnic University	1
12=	Aston	1
12=	Glamorgan	1
12=	Huddersfield	1
12=	Hull	1
12=	Loughborough	1
12=	Sheffield	1
12=	Strathclyde	1
12=	York	1
21=	Birmingham	0
21=	Glasgow	0
21=	Hertfordshire	0
21=	Manchester Metropolitan	0
21=	Surrey	0
21=	Teesside	0
27=	Aberdeen	-1

Rank	University	Value Added (ave=o)
27=	Dundee	-1
27=	Leicester	-1
27=	Liverpool	-1
27=	Queen Mary & Westfield College London	-1
27=	Newcastle upon Tyne	-1
27=	Nottingham Trent	-1
27=	Reading	-1
35=	Bradford	-2
35=	Keele	-2
35=	St Andrews	-2
35=	Southampton	-2
35=	Stirling	-2
40=	Bath	-4
40=	Belfast	-4
40=	University College London	-4
40=	University of Wales Bangor	-4
40=	University of Wales Cardiff	-4
45=	Bristol	-5
45=	East Anglia	-5
45=	Exeter	-5
45=	Kent	-5
45=	Kings College London	-5
45=	Oxford	-5
45=	Sussex	-5
52=	Durham	-6
52=	Warwick	-6
54	University of Wales Swansea	-7

NOTE Value-added calculations are based on the single reference course Chemistry F100. Only institutions offering this course are ranked.

If, by now, further proof were needed that UMIST is the Westlife of the science and technology subjects then this table is it. Throughout this year's survey UMIST has scored number one after number one in the technical areas and now follows a second place in the main science ranking with top spot according to value-added. With the exception of UMIST, its neighbours in Manchester and Nottingham, the top ten by value-added do not appear in the top ten by employability points – a pattern repeated in most subject areas.

Further comments and selected quotes

This is now the third successive year that **Cambridge** has headed the list of employers' favourites in this subject. **UMIST**, now second, was number one in 1998.

Although not making an impact on the top ten risers, there have been significant moves since 1998 for **Nottingham** (up seven places) and **Sheffield** (up eight places) into this year's top ten.

Of the four universities sharing tenth spot, **Bristol**, **Glasgow** and **Heriot-Watt** record rises since 1998. Heriot-Watt's progress has been relentless over this period, moving from 25th, through 24th, 21st equal and 18th equal to where it is today.

Though not naming the specific institutions they avoid, one small company, basing its perceptions on course content and rigour of awards, avoids *'many of the polys upgraded to universities'*.

Meanwhile, a recruiter in the Midlands singles out an individual course for a special mention, namely, **Sheffield Hallam**'s *'excellent food science graduates'*.

And if there is still doubt that graduate recruitment practices are influenced by perceptions of specific universities and colleges, the following quotes should clear matters up. One recruiter, who selects many science graduates every year, refers to companies' *'high opinion of the science department at Bristol'*. Another, based in London and operating mainly in the subject, especially targets **Oxford** because of, simply, *'reputation'*.

SOCIAL SCIENCE/ECONOMICS

Employability rankings summary

Total votes: 134
Universities ranked: 76   **Not ranked:** 21
Highest: Oxford (9 points)   **Lowest:** Luton/Thames Valley (-4 points)

Recruiters' perceptions of higher education and graduates

Influence of university reputation

	Social Science/ Economics %	All replies %
Total	0.0	0.5
Considerable	17.6	19.9
Somewhat	35.3	39.8
Slight	23.5	19.4
None	23.5	20.4

Just over half the recruiters (52.9 per cent) of social science and economics graduates surveyed are somewhat or considerably influenced by their opinion of a university when selecting candidates for employment. Moreover, more than three-quarters are at least slightly influenced. When compared with the general case, however, it appears that social science/economics recruiters are slightly less influenced by university reputation.

Changing degree standards

	Social Science/ Economics %	All replies %
Falling	16.7	13.4
Falling slightly	27.8	39.3
No change	44.4	40.3
Rising slightly	11.1	7.0
Rising	0.0	0.0

Recruiters in this subject seem to have a slightly better opinion of current degree standards than average. Having said this, almost half (44.5 per cent) still believe that standards are falling, at least slightly.

New graduates' employability

	Social Science/ Economics %	All replies %
Good	23.5	20.0
Fairly good	58.8	59.5
No view	5.9	8.8
Fairly poor	11.8	11.7
Poor	0.0	0.0

In this, the final subject area of our report, it is not a surprise to find that the majority of employers regard their new graduate recruits' employability as being at least fairly good. In fact, four out of five believe this to be the case while only 11.8 per cent take an opposing stance.

Preferences for employability qualities

Rank	Employability qualities	Social Science/ Economics %	All replies %
1=	A-level grades	77.8	53.7
1=	Enthusiasm	77.8	81.5
3	Business awareness	72.2	62.5
4=	Teamworking	66.7	66.7
4=	Numeracy	66.7	64.8
6=	Degree classification	61.1	67.6
6=	Work experience	61.1	69.9
6=	Verbal communication skills	61.1	83.8
9=	Computing skills	55.6	59.3
9=	Personal/transferable skills	55.6	66.7
9=	Written communication skills	55.6	71.8
12	Self-reliance	50.0	54.2
13	Problem solving	36.4	66.9
14=	Sports & hobbies	33.3	27.3
14=	Sandwich course	33.3	31.5

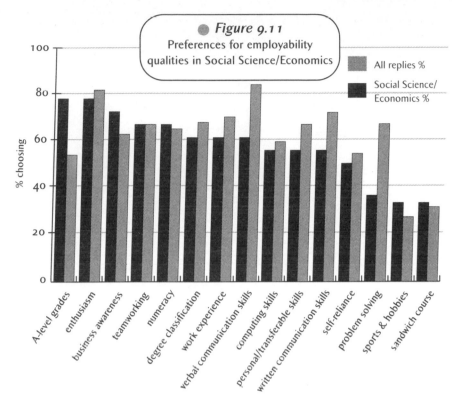

Figure 9.11
Preferences for employability qualities in Social Science/Economics

Legend:
- All replies %
- Social Science/Economics %

y-axis: % choosing (0 to 100)

x-axis categories: A-level grades, enthusiasm, business awareness, teamworking, numeracy, degree classification, work experience, verbal communication skills, computing skills, personal/transferable skills, written communication skills, self-reliance, problem solving, sports & hobbies, sandwich course

A number of qualities receive relatively little backing here. Most notably, verbal and written communication skills drop a long way down the list, while problem solving does particularly badly with only 36.4 per cent support. The latter can perhaps be explained if you consider that this subject area is not particularly technical. The relatively good showings for A-level results and sports and hobbies, on the other hand, suggest that employers of social science and economics graduates value breadth of knowledge and personality in their recruits. Business awareness also does well in comparison with the results for all subjects, possibly because the world of business is a popular destination for graduates in this subject area.

RANKING OF UNIVERSITIES BY EMPLOYABILITY POINTS ••••

Rank	University	Employability points
1	Oxford	9
2	Bristol	8
3	Southampton	8
4=	Cambridge	7
4=	London School of Economics	7
6	Reading	6
7	Warwick	6
8=	Edinburgh	5
8=	Manchester	5
8=	Nottingham	5
11	Sheffield	4
12	Heriot-Watt	4
13=	Bath	3
13=	Birmingham	3
13=	Durham	3
13=	Leeds	3
13=	Royal Holloway London	3
13=	York	3
19	Hull	2
20=	City	2
20=	Essex	2
20=	Exeter	2
20=	Queen Mary & Westfield College London	2
20=	University College London	2
20=	Newcastle upon Tyne	2
20=	Portsmouth	2
20=	St Andrews	2
20=	South Bank	2
20=	University of Wales Bangor	2
20=	University of Wales Cardiff	2
20=	University of Wales Swansea	2
32=	Lancaster	1
32=	Imperial College London	1
32=	Kings College London	1
35=	London Guildhall	1
36	Brunel	-1
37=	Bradford	-1

Rank	University	Employability points
37=	Sussex	-1
39=	Anglia Polytechnic University	-2
39=	Brighton	-2
39=	Buckingham	-2
39=	Central England	-2
39=	Central Lancashire	-2
39=	De Montfort	-2
39=	Derby	-2
39=	Glamorgan	-2
39=	Glasgow Caledonian	-2
39=	Hertfordshire	-2
39=	Huddersfield	-2
39=	Leeds Metropolitan	-2
39=	Lincoln	-2
39=	Liverpool John Moores	-2
39=	Manchester Metropolitan	-2
39=	Napier	-2
39=	Northumbria	-2
39=	Nottingham Trent	-2
39=	Paisley	-2
39=	Robert Gordon	-2
39=	Salford	-2
39=	Sheffield Hallam	-2
39=	Staffordshire	-2
39=	Teesside	-2
39=	Ulster	-2
39=	University of Wales Lampeter	-2
39=	West of England	-2
66=	Bournemouth	-3
66=	East London	-3
66=	Greenwich	-3
66=	Middlesex	-3
66=	North London	-3
66=	Plymouth	-3
66=	Sunderland	-3
66=	Westminster	-3
66=	Wolverhampton	-3
75=	Luton	-4
75=	Thames Valley	-4

The risers and fallers

TOP TEN RISERS

Rank 2002	University	Rank 1998	Changes
13=	Leeds	49	26▲
13=	Royal Holloway London	40=	27▲
20=	City	40=	20▲
20=	Newcastle upon Tyne	40=	20▲
8=	Nottingham	28=	20▲
12	Heriot-Watt	28=	16▲
11	Sheffield	26=	15▲
6	Reading	20=	14▲
13/39/39	Bath/Buckingham/Derby	26/52/52	13▲
39=	De Montfort/Hertfordshire	52=	13▲

'TOP' TEN FALLERS

Rank 2002	University	Rank 1998	Changes
39=	Manchester Metropolitan/Napier/ Northumbria	28=	11▼
39=	Nottingham Trent/Teesside	28=	11▼
66=	East London	52=	14▼
66=	North London	52=	14▼
32=	Lancaster	11=	21▼
32=	Kings College London	11=	21▼
39=	Sheffield Hallam	16=	23▼
75=	Thames Valley	51	24▼
66=	Bournemouth	28=	38▼
66=	Plymouth	28=	38▼

On this occasion, the Russell Group takes control of the top ten, but Reading, the lone outsider, steals a march by rising 14 places since 1998 to sixth position. This makes it the eighth biggest climber. Many of the other top ten risers have made the most of their good fortune by surging into the top 20 – maybe next year we will see the likes of Heriot-Watt and City break up the big boys' top ten party.

There is just enough space to include an honourable mention for South Bank, which does not often appear in lists of favoured universities in any subjects, but here it appears in a respectable joint 20th position.

RANKING OF UNIVERSITIES BY VALUE-ADDED

Rank	University	Value Added (ave=0)
1	Abertay	8
2=	Heriot-Watt	6
2=	London Guildhall	6
4	Teesside	5
5=	Anglia Polytechnic University	4
5=	Coventry	4
5=	Lincoln	4
5=	Staffordshire	4
9=	East London	3
9=	Liverpool John Moores	3
9=	Northumbria	3
12=	Bristol	2
12=	Buckingham	2
12=	Central England	2
12=	De Montfort	2
12=	Huddersfield	2
12=	Kingston	2
12=	Portsmouth	2
12=	Reading	2
12=	Southampton	2
12=	University of Wales Bangor	2
22=	Middlesex	1
22=	Plymouth	1
22=	University of Wales Aberystwyth	1
25=	Aberdeen	0
25=	City	0
25=	Dundee	0
25=	Hull	0
25=	Queen Mary & Westfield College London	0

Rank	University	Value Added (ave=0)
25=	Manchester	0
25=	Sheffield	0
32	Nottingham Trent	-1
33=	Essex	-2
33=	Leicester	-2
33=	Liverpool	-2
33=	Manchester Metropolitan	-2
33=	Newcastle upon Tyne	-2
33=	St Andrews	-2
33=	Ulster	-2
40=	Bath	-3
40=	Birmingham	-3
40=	Bradford	-3
40=	Brunel	-3
40=	East Anglia	-3
40=	Edinburgh	-3
40=	Leeds	-3
40=	University of Wales Cardiff	-3
40=	West of England	-3
40=	York	-3
50=	Belfast	-4
50=	Cambridge	-4
50=	Exeter	-4
50=	Kent	-4
50=	Loughborough	-4
50=	Nottingham Trent	-4
50=	Salford	-4
50=	Warwick	-4
58=	Durham	-5
58=	Lancaster	-5
60	University College London	-8

Note Value-added calculations are based on the single reference course Economics L100. Only institutions offering this course are ranked.

The older universities suffer here by virtue of their relatively tough entry requirements, leaving the path clear for the new universities and former polytechnics to shine. In particular, after making good progress over the last three years in the main ranking, Heriot-Watt also shows what it can do on the value-added front by making second place. It is beaten to the top spot by Abertay, which easily pulls off its highest value-added position of this year's survey.

Further comments and selected quotes

It was first in 1998 and is first again this year, but **Oxford** has spent the last couple of years as runner-up to **Bristol**, which now drops to second.

Leeds, the biggest climber, is described by one major firm, which recruits exclusively in this subject, as being *'particularly good/underrated'*.

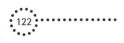

Bottom overall are **Luton** and **Thames Valley**. A London firm, counting itself as considerably influenced by its rating of a university, has a *'preference for 15 targeted universities'* but identifies Luton as having a *'poor reputation'*.

One recruiter for a high street bank specifies 14 universities from which they are likely to select graduates. Most top 20 institutions are included among their favourites but **Cambridge**, **London School of Economics** and **Manchester** are not.

Caution: The scale of graduate recruitment is low relative to other areas surveyed. This means relatively few active recruiters, votes, opinions and providers, and that a handful of votes can make a considerable difference to the rankings.

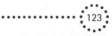

10. Summary of Rankings

The following table summarises the performance of each university included in our survey. It lists their ranking by employability points for all subjects. If a university did not receive a subject-specific nomination then they appear as *not ranked* (*n/r*).

This table is a useful illustration of how the quality of institutions varies across subjects but it also provides an impression of which are generally perceived as being good. However, you should not take it to be the last word. Read through the subject tables again and think about the value that each institution might add to you. Use this table only as *part* of your research.

TABLE 10.1 SUMMARY OF UNIVERSITIES' EMPLOYABILITY RANKINGS, BY SUBJECT

University	Bus	Civ Eng	Com /IT	Elc Eng	Fin	Gen Eng	Lang	Law	Math	Sci	Soc Sci
Universities ranked	96	72	77	73	53	82	97	47	52	54	75
Aberdeen	n/r	24=	40=	37=	n/r	36=	27=	28=	25=	35=	n/r
Abertay	51=	69=	40=	37=	n/r	46=	63=	n/r	n/r	n/r	n/r
University of Wales Aberystwyth	73=	53=	40=	37=	24=	n/r	63=	25=	n/r	35=	n/r
Anglia Polytechnic University	63=	38=	n/r	56=	n/r	69=	63=	n/r	n/r	54=	39=
Aston	4=	24=	6	16	17=	14	10=	n/r	52=	35=	n/r
University of Wales Bangor	41	n/r	n/r	n/r	17=	n/r	27=	n/r	n/r	n/r	20=
Bath	6	6=	18=	12	11=	6	9	n/r	41=	30=	13=
Belfast	30=	38=	40=	14	24=	28	27=	28=	41=	47=	n/r
Birmingham	7	2	3=	3	7	7	16=	13=	21	8	13=
Bournemouth	24	n/r	40=	n/r	19=	n/r	16=	n/r	n/r	n/r	66=
Bradford	46=	n/r	67	37=	42	26=	10=	n/r	25=	35=	37=
Brighton	16	71	n/r	37=	24=	55=	58=	n/r	n/r	n/r	39=
Bristol	8=	10=	3=	7=	4	11	16=	5=	15	10=	2
Brunel	42	31	9=	4	n/r	8	27=	n/r	16=	16=	36
Buckingham	88=	67=	n/r	n/r	n/r	n/r	63=	n/r	n/r	n/r	39=
Cambridge	8=	28=	2	5	23	5	1	2	1	1	4=
University of Wales Cardiff	25=	3	23=	29=	24=	29=	27=	12	25=	n/r	20=
Central England	68=	38=	61=	56=	24=	78=	63=	n/r	50=	54=	39=
Central Lancashire	73=	n/r	n/r	n/r	n/r	n/r	58=	n/r	n/r	n/r	39=
City	46=	38=	40=	70	36=	77	27=	n/r	n/r	n/r	20=
Coventry	46=	32=	40=	35	n/r	67=	63=	n/r	n/r	n/r	n/r
De Montfort	38=	n/r	17	56=	n/r	82	27=	46	44=	35=	39=
Derby	88=	n/r	40=	56=	n/r	69=	97	n/r	n/r	54=	39=
Dundee	73=	38=	40=	n/r	n/r	n/r	27=	n/r	n/r	n/r	n/r
Durham	25=	20=	23=	25=	24=	23	4	9=	3	30=	13=
East Anglia	73=	n/r	70=	n/r	n/r	55=	16=	13=	n/r	n/r	n/r

University	Bus	Civ Eng	Com /IT	Elc Eng	Fin	Gen Eng	Lang	Law	Math	Sci	Soc Sci
East London	92=	67=	70=	56=	n/r	60=	63=	n/r	n/r	n/r	66=
Edinburgh	30=	14=	9-	13	n/r	17	3	41=	25=	14=	8=
Essex	30=	n/r	n/r	37=	24=	46=	63=	n/r	n/r	n/r	20=
Exeter	22=	24=	61=	29=	6	29=	5=	9=	22=	n/r	20=
Glamorgan	73=	n/r	40=	37=	n/r	n/r	63=	28=	n/r	n/r	39=
Glasgow	66=	53=	18=	22=	n/r	22	16=	41=	11=	10=	n/r
Glasgow Caledonian	68=	69=	n/r	n/r	n/r	46=	63=	41=	n/r	n/r	39=
Goldsmiths College London	68=	n/r	n/r	n/r	n/r	n/r	27=	28=	n/r	n/r	n/r
Greenwich	73=	38=	n/r	n/r	n/r	60=	63=	n/r	25=	n/r	66=
Heriot-Watt	63=	5	18=	9	19=	12	27=	n/r	25=	10=	12
Hertfordshire	72	n/r	69	37=	n/r	26=	63=	n/r	25=	35=	39=
Huddersfield	38=	n/r	n/r	72	n/r	74	27=	28=	n/r	n/r	39-
Hull	11=	38=	61=	19=	11=	29=	16=	13=	n/r	16=	19
Imperial College London	35=	23	7=	2	24=	3	27=	13=	16=	4	32=
Keele	51=	53=	n/r	56=	n/r	60=	27=	n/r	n/r	30=	n/r
Kent	51=	n/r	40=	n/r	n/r	55=	58=	n/r	25=	n/r	n/r
Kings College London	48=	32=	29=	22=	36=	39=	27=	5=	41=	30=	32=
Kingston	17=	38=	66	56=	46=	59	63=	n/r	n/r	35=	n/r
University of Wales Lampeter	73=	n/r	n/r	n/r	n/r	n/r	63=	n/r	n/r	n/r	39=
Lancaster	13	53=	40=	37=	44=	39=	10=	28=	47=	n/r	32=
Leeds	2=	4	12=	25=	10	18	5=	28=	13=	10=	13=
Leeds Metropolitan	11=	n/r	67=	56=	43	78=	63=	n/r	25=	n/r	39=
Leicester	51=	32=	n/r	n/r	n/r	n/r	27=	13-	n/r	23=	n/r
Lincoln	73=	n/r	n/r	56=	n/r	78=	63=	47=	n/r	n/r	39=
Liverpool	35=	19	33=	25=	n/r	21	56	28=	n/r	23=	n/r
Liverpool John Moores	34	38=	33=	73	22	78=	63-	n/r	16=	n/r	39=
London Guildhall	92=	n/r	n/r	n/r	46=	n/r	27=	28=	n/r	35=	35=
London School of Economics	14	53=	37=	n/r	3	n/r	16=	3=	46	n/r	4=
Loughborough	15	1	23=	15	11=	2	27=	25=	n/r	16=	n/r
Luton	96	35=	70=	71	52=	60=	95=	44=	50=	52=	75=
Manchester	4=	13	3=	19=	2	9=	16	8	8=	3	8=
Manchester Metropolitan	58=	n/r	39	37=	n/r	46=	63=	n/r	52=	54=	39=
Middlesex	87	53=	40=	n/r	n/r	60=	63=	n/r	n/r	n/r	66=
Napier	68=	51=	40=	37=	n/r	36=	63=	n/r	25=	35=	39=
Newcastle upon Tyne	40	14=	29=	37=	11-	20	63=	25=	6	23=	20=
North London	95	n/r	n/r	n/r	n/r	n/r	63=	n/r	n/r	n/r	66=
Northumbria	65	n/r	40=	n/r	51	46=	57	28=	n/r	n/r	39=
Nottingham	2=	12	11	10=	8	4	5=	13=	5	5	8=
Nottingham Trent	29	20=	29=	36	24=	25	27=	28=	25=	n/r	39=
Oxford	10	28=	12=	17	16	15	2	1	2	6=	1
Oxford Brookes	20=	37	77	52=	n/r	39=	27=	n/r	25=	n/r	n/r

University	Bus	Civ Eng	Com /IT	Elc Eng	Fin	Gen Eng	Lang	Law	Math	Sci	Soc Sci
Paisley	73=	51=	40=	37=	n/r	39=	63=	n/r	n/r	35=	39=
Plymouth	25=	24=	40=	25=	n/r	54	10=	n/r	25=	23=	66=
Portsmouth	30=	18	37=	22=	39=	44=	27=	n/r	n/r	34	20=
Queen Mary & Westfield College London	51=	n/r	70=	56=	n/r	60=	27=	9=	16=	23=	20=
Reading	25=	32=	18=	56=	9	69=	16=	13=	52=	23=	6
Robert Gordon	73=	63=	n/r	n/r	n/r	36=	63=	n/r	n/r	35=	39=
Royal Holloway London	73=	n/r	n/r	n/r	n/r	n/r	27=	n/r	n/r	n/r	13=
St Andrews	73=	62	40=	29=	n/r	39=	8	13=	13=	19=	20=
Salford	43=	20=	n/r	29=	n/r	24	27=	n/r	n/r	23=	39=
Sheffield	20=	6=	15	10=	19=	13	10=	13=	8=	9	11
Sheffield Hallam	43=	28=	29=	55	n/r	67=	27=	47=	25=	46	39=
Southampton	17=	10=	16	7=	5	19	63=	3=	7	19=	3
South Bank	73=	72	70=	56=	n/r	75=	63=	n/r	n/r	54=	20=
Staffordshire	92=	n/r	23=	56=	n/r	75=	63=	n/r	n/r	n/r	39=
Stirling	62	53=	n/r	29=	11=	34=	16=	n/r	20	47=	n/r
Strathclyde	46=	14=	18=	6	n/r	9=	27=	n/r	25=	6=	n/r
Sunderland	88=	n/r	40=	n/r	46=	n/r	63=	n/r	n/r	n/r	66=
Surrey	35=	8	40=	52=	24=	29=	63=	n/r	22=	22	n/r
Sussex	51=	53=	61=	n/r	24=	69=	58=	28=	n/r	n/r	37=
University of Wales Swansea	58=	53=	61=	52=	24=	46=	27=	28=	25=	n/r	20=
Teesside	88=	38=	70=	n/r	46=	46=	63=	n/r	n/r	n/r	39=
Thames Valley	61	65=	70=	56=	52=	60=	95=	44=	44=	52=	75=
Ulster	66=	38=	33=	n/r	n/r	44=	27=	n/r	49	47=	39=
UMIST	19	9	1	1	36=	1	63=	n/r	11=	2	n/r
University College London	22=	38=	23=	29=	36=	34=	16=	13=	22=	19=	20=
Warwick	1	14=	7=	18	1	16	10=	5=	4	47=	7
Westminster	51=	n/r	33=	37=	46=	55=	27=	n/r	47=	47=	66=
West of England	60	38=	23=	37=	44=	46=	27=	13=	n/r	n/r	39=
Wolverhampton	73=	63=	40=	n/r	n/r	69=	63=	n/r	n/r	n/r	66=
York	46=	32=	12=	19=	36=	29=	58=	13=	8=	14=	13=

Finally, we have a table revealing how each university's status has changed over the last three years. For this year and 1998 we have added up all the points and votes each institution was awarded to produce two 'ultimate' aggregate rankings. These rankings are not helpful in themselves but, given that the subject areas remain unchanged, the difference between them should indicate how recruiters' perceptions of each university are changing over time. For instance, Cambridge has experienced no change in aggregate rank since 1998, meaning that recruiters remain consistent in their general belief that Cambridge produces highly employable graduates. De Montfort, on the other hand, has risen 38 places in the aggregate rankings, suggesting that employers are gradually holding the former polytechnic in higher regard as time goes on.

TABLE 10.2 CHANGE IN AGGREGATE RANKINGS OF UNIVERSITIES SIINCE 1998

University	Change in aggregate ranking (1998-2002)
Aberdeen	17 ▼
Abertay	6 ▼
University of Wales Aberystwyth	9 ▲
Anglia Polytechnic University	3 ▼
Aston	2 ▲
University of Wales Bangor	26 ▲
Bath	no change
Belfast	19 ▲
Birmingham	no change
Bournemouth	19 ▲
Bradford	8 ▼
Brighton	6 ▲
Bristol	2 ▲
Brunel	8 ▲
Buckingham	7 ▲
Cambridge	no change
University of Wales Cardiff	26 ▲
Central England	2 ▲
Central Lancashire	13 ▲
City	17 ▼
Coventry	10 ▲
De Montfort	38 ▲
Derby	5 ▲
Dundee	33 ▼
Durham	no change
East Anglia	10 ▼
East London	no change
Edinburgh	9 ▼
Essex	16 ▲
Exeter	1 ▼
Glamorgan	6 ▲
Glasgow	7 ▼
Glasgow Caledonian	32 ▼
Goldsmiths College London	5 ▲
Greenwich	4 ▲
Heriot Watt	1 ▼
Hertfordshire	5 ▲
Huddersfield	11 ▲
Hull	7 ▲
Imperial College London	2 ▼
Keele	2 ▼
Kent	9 ▼
Kings College London	1 ▼
Kingston	13 ▼

University	Change in aggregate ranking (1998-2002)
University of Wales Lampeter	1 ▲
Lancaster	3 ▲
Leeds	5 ▼
Leeds Metropolitan	14 ▼
Leicester	9 ▲
Lincoln	9 ▼
Liverpool	5 ▼
Liverpool John Moores	2 ▼
London Guildhall	2 ▲
London School of Economics	2 ▼
Loughborough	1 ▲
Luton	5 ▼
Manchester	1 ▼
Manchester Metropolitan	36 ▼
Middlesex	4 ▼
Napier	4 ▼
Newcastle upon Tyne	1 ▲
North London	2 ▼
Northumbria	24 ▼
Nottingham	13 ▲
Nottingham Trent	13 ▲
Oxford	5 ▼
Oxford Brookes	36 ▲
Paisley	7 ▲
Plymouth	18 ▲
Portsmouth	22 ▲
Queen Mary & Westfield College London	1 ▲
Reading	no change
Robert Gordon	7 ▼
Royal Holloway London	1 ▲
St Andrews	6 ▼
Salford	1 ▲
Sheffield	2 ▲
Sheffield Hallam	21 ▼
Southampton	4 ▼
South Bank	8 ▼
Staffordshire	8 ▼
Stirling	7 ▼
Strathclyde	5 ▼
Sunderland	13 ▼
Surrey	2 ▲
Sussex	24 ▼
University of Wales Swansea	18 ▲

University	Change in aggregate ranking (1998-2002)
Teesside	35 ▼
Thames Valley	4 ▼
Ulster	9 ▲
UMIST	2 ▲
University College London	1 ▲

University	Change in aggregate ranking (1998-2002)
Warwick	8 ▲
Westminster	▲ 18
West of England	no change
Wolverhampton	3 ▼
York	6 ▲

NOTE A rise/fall in aggregate ranking does not necessarily mean that the recruiters' opinion of that institution has improved/lessened – it is an indication of each university's relative status only.

FINAL THOUGHTS

Our concluding comments are echoed throughout this book: students put a lot of time, effort and money into going to university or college, and when they come out at the other end they enter into a highly competitive world of work. Students therefore need to know where and how they can become best prepared for life as a graduate employee. The recruiters who select graduates have given us their views; and we have passed them on to you.

Nothing in this book is prescriptive. We only mean to provide you with some impartial information and a few ideas for you to use as you research your options more thoroughly. There are a number of useful address and resources listed on pages 129–39 to help you in this task.

We like to think our surveys are helpful. If you have any comments or criticisms, let us know. Our work is ongoing and suggestions for future editions are always welcome. You can contact us by emailing authors@careers-portal.co.uk.

11. Further Resources and Useful Addresses

Visit our companion website www.careers-portal.co.uk/earning for more on our survey and data as well as for useful information and links relating to the issues of higher education and graduate employability and an explanation of the Teaching Quality Assessments written by John Randle, former Chief Executive of the QAA.

We have also put together a list of books, addresses and websites that you might find useful in becoming an employable graduate. It is by no means comprehensive but is plenty to be getting on with.

Higher Education

BOOKS

Choosing Your Degree Course & University (Trotman)
Brian Heap
0 85660 740 1
£18.99
Advice on how to choose and judge your degree course and how they differ between institutions.

The Complete Guide Series 2003 (UCAS/Trotman)
A series of course directories providing details of all degree courses within a number of subject areas, using information taken from the UCAS database.

Art & Design
Courses
0 85660 815 7
£14.99

Computer Science
Courses
0 85660 806 8
£14.99

Healthcare
Professions
Courses
0 85660 807 6
£12.99

Physical Science
Courses
0 85660 808 4
£14.99

Business Courses
0 85660 804 1
£14.99

Engineering
Courses
0 85660 816 5
£14.99

Performing Arts
Courses
0 85660 805 X
£12.99

Degree Course Offers 2003 Entry (Trotman)
Brian Heap
0 85660 756 8
£22.99
Reference guide listing target offers in terms of the new UCAS tariff, with additional grade or specific point information. Helps students to choose universities and colleges best suited to their chances of success.

Directory of University & College Entry 2003–4 (Trotman)
0 85660 799 1
£32.99
Comprehensive directory of UK higher education courses. It groups similar courses together to help readers compare entry requirements at a glance and make a shortlist of institutions to apply to.

The Disabled Students' Guide to University (Trotman)
Emma Caprez
0 85660 704 5
£14.99
Helps prospective students choose the right university by providing them with details on disabled provision in all aspects of higher education life.

The Student Book 2003 (Trotman)
Klaus Boehm & Jenny Lees-Spalding
0 85660 758 4
£14.99
A one-stop applicant's guide to higher education, providing honest and down-to-earth opinions of what student life at each university and college in the UK is really like.

University & College Entrance: The Official Guide 2003 Entry (a.k.a. The Big Guide) (UCAS)
1 84361 007 8
£24.95
Published by UCAS, the Big Guide is a directory of all UK degree and HND courses at publicly funded institutions.

UCAS/Universities Scotland: Entrance to Higher Education in Scotland 2003 (UCAS)
1 84361 006 X
£8.95
Directory of higher education choices in Scotland, listing degree and diploma courses available in Scottish universities and colleges.

ADDRESSES

Higher Education Statistics Agency
18 Royal Crescent
Cheltenham
Gloucestershire GL50 3DA
customer.services@hesa.ac.uk
www.hesa.ac.uk

National Union of Students
Nelson Mandela House
461 Holloway Road
London N7 6LJ
020 7272 8900
nusuk@nus.org.uk
www.nus.org.uk

Quality Assurance Agency for Higher Education
Southgate House
Southgate Street
Gloucester GL1 1UB
01452 557 000
comms@qaa.ac.uk
www.qaa.org.uk

Universities and Colleges Admissions Service (UCAS)
Rosehill
New Barn Lane
Cheltenham
Gloucestershire GL52 3LZ
1242 222444
enq@ucas.ac.uk
www.ucas.com

WEBSITES

www.careers-portal.co.uk
Profiles UK universities as well as offering advice on choosing a degree course.

www.hero.ac.uk
Higher Education & Research Opportunities – the official gateway site to the UK's universities, colleges and research organisations.

www.thecoursesource.co.uk
An index to all UK degree courses, searchable by a range of criteria – subject, region, college or university, and at undergraduate or postgraduate levels.

Graduate Careers

BOOKS

The Art of Building Windmills – Career Tactics for the 21st Century
Dr Peter Hawkins
0 9535980 0 4
£12.99
Clear guidance to help graduates effectively manage their careers.

The Graduate Career Handbook (FT Prentice Hall)
Shirley Jenner
0 273 64428 9
£18.99
An interactive, fully web-referenced career guide and job-hunting companion for university students.

Hobsons Graduate Career Directory 2003 (Hobsons)
1 86017 945 2
£20.99
Lists more than 60,000 vacancies and graduate courses, indexed by degree subject, occupation and employer type.

The Times Graduate Job Hunting Guide (Kogan Page)
Mark Parkinson
0 7494 3418 X
£8.99
Guides graduates through the application maze and provides practical advice on how to get the job they really want.

What Do Graduates Do? 2002 (CSU/UCAS)
1 84016 084 5
£9.95
Contains the latest statistics on the employment of new graduates but only six months after graduation.

ADDRESSES

Association of Graduate Recruiters
Innovation Centre
Warwick Technology Park
Gallows Hill
Warwick CV34 6UW
01926 623 236
info@agr.org.uk
www.agr.org.uk

Higher Education Careers Services Unit
Prospects House
Booth Street East
Manchester M13 9EP
0161 277 5200
comments@csu.ac.uk
www.prospects.csu.ac.uk

www.agcas.org.uk
Association of Graduate Careers Advisory Services – the professional association for careers services in higher education.

http://cando.lancs.ac.uk
Careers site for graduates with disabilities.

www.doctorjob.com
Comprehensive graduate careers website.

www.gradunet.co.uk
Gradunet – virtual careers office.

Skills & Employability

BOOKS

Boosting Your Career Prospects – A Student Guide (Trotman)
Peter Hawkins
0 85660 298 1
£8.99
Guide to developing employability skills at university.

Developing Your Employment Skills (Trotman)
Val Foster
0 85660 308 2
£8.99
An exploration of skills and employment.

Enhancing Your Employability (How To Books)
Roderic Ashley
1 85703 371 X
£9.99
Offers guidance and ideas about how you can enhance your own prospects of working in a sphere you enjoy by identifying and developing your strengths and skills, and overcoming your weaknesses.

Projecting Your Skills at Work (Trotman)
Polly Bird
0 85660 462 3
£8.99
Guide to career management full of practical advice on how to develop your career and get recognition for your skills.

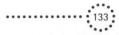

Q&A World of Work Series (Trotman)
These books offer a basic but advice-packed approach to workplace skills.

Business Etiquette
0 85660 329 5
£4.99

Business Letter Writing
0 85660 326 0
£4.99

Presentations
0 85660 327 9
£4.99

Telephoning
0 85660 325 2
£4.99

Time Management
0 85660 328 7
£4.99

ADDRESSES

The Centre for Recording Achievement
39 Bridgeman Terrace
Wigan WN1 1TT
01942 826 761
enquiries@recordingachievement.org
www.recordingachievement.org

City & Guilds
1 Giltspur Street
London EC1A 9DD
020 7294 2800
enquiry@city-and-guilds.co.uk
www.city-and-guilds.co.uk

Edexcel
0870 240 9800
enquiries@edexcel.org.uk
www.edexcel.org.uk

Graduate Into Employment Unit
Cathedral Precinct
Mount Pleasant
Liverpool L3 5TQ
0800 018 6925
www.gieu.co.uk

Sector Skills Development Agency
Room E4c
Moorfoot
Sheffield S1 4PQ
0870 000 2399
ssda.info@dfes.gsi.gov.uk
www.ssda.org.uk

WEBSITES

www.windmillsprogramme.com
Virtual career coach to help you with managing your career.

www.nusonline.co.uk/nslp
National Student Learning Programme – training in key skills for students.

Gap Year

BOOKS

Before You Go – The Ultimate Guide to Planning Your Gap Year (Quiller Press)
Tom Griffiths
1 90401 201 9
£7.95
Includes an A-Z guide to issues affecting travellers, from drugs to diet and first aid to photography.

The Gap Year Guidebook (John Catt Educational Ltd)
0 901577 69 3
£11.95
Covers advice and information on further study, job opportunities, useful contacts, voluntary work and expeditions, paid work in the UK and abroad and feedback from students who have experienced gap years.

Making the Most of Your Gap Year (Trotman)
Margaret Flynn
0 85660 831 9
£1 (available only in batches of ten or more)
This guide is designed to help students in the sixth form decide whether to take a gap year and if so, provides advice on how they can spend it.

Taking a Year Off (Trotman)
Val Butcher
0 85660 552 2
£9.99
Helps those considering a gap year to make the best use of their time. It also explores employers' and admissions tutors' attitudes to a year out.

Taking a Year Out (How To Books)
Nick Vandome
1 85703 764 2
£9.99
Contains details of over 220 contact organisations as well as valuable advice on health and safety and guidance on using the Internet for research.

Working Holidays Abroad (Trotman)
Mark Hempshell
0 85660 467 4
£9.99
This excellent travel guide is full of ideas for jobs, useful tips and dos and don'ts of travelling.

Work Your Way Around the World (Vacation Work Publications)
Susan Griffith
1 85458 251 8
£12.95
This guide for the working traveller incorporates hundreds of first-hand accounts to offer advice on how to find work around the world in advance or on the spot.

ADDRESSES

BUNAC – Working Adventures Worldwide
16 Bowling Green Lane
London EC1R 0QH
020 7251 3472
enquiries@bunac.org.uk
www.bunac.org

Camp America
37a Queen's Gate
London SW7 5HR
020 7581 7373
enquiries@campamerica.co.uk
www.campamerica.co.uk

i-to-i – TEFL training and volunteer placements
9 Blenheim Terrace
Leeds LS2 9HZ
0870 333 2332
www.i-to-i.com

Quest Overseas
32 Clapham Mansions
Nightingale Lane
London SW4 9AQ
020 8673 3313
www.questoverseas.com

Raleigh International
27 Parsons Green Lane
London SW6 4HZ
020 7371 8585
www.raleigh.org.uk

Voluntary Service Overseas (VSO)
317 Putney Bridge Road
London SW15 2PN
020 8780 7200
www.vso.org.uk

WEBSITES

www.gapyear.com
Gap year community website.

www.gap-year.com
Comprehensive gap year information.

Work Experience

BOOKS

International Voluntary Work (Vacation Work Publications)
Victoria Pybus
1 85458 279 8
£11.95
New edition of the book that covers all types of voluntary work all over the world.

Summer Jobs Abroad 2002 (Vacation Work Publications)
Ian Collier & David Woodworth
1 85458 260 7
£9.99
Contains details of over 30,000 vacancies in more than 50 countries.

Summer Jobs Britain 2002 (Vacation Work Publications)
Andrew Jones & David Woodworth
1 85458 263 1
£9.99
Lists over 30,000 vacancies offering salaries of up to £300 per week.

Working in the Voluntary Sector (How To Books)
Craig Brown
1 85703 629 8
£9.99
Lists nearly 250 valuable contacts and practical tips.

Making Work Experience Count (How To Books)
Sally Longson
1 85703 517 8
£9.99
Helps you identify exactly what you want to achieve and how to assess what you have learned.

ADDRESSES

Community Service Volunteers
237 Pentonville Road
London N1 9NJ
020 7278 6601
information@csv.org.uk
www.csv.org.uk

Shell Technology Enterprise Programme (STEP)
Head Office
Harling House
62 Copperfield Street
London SE1 0DJ
020 7921 5450
enquiries@step.org.uk
www.step.org.uk

The Year in Industry
University of Manchester
Simon Building
Oxford Road
Manchester M13 9PL
enquiries@yini.org.uk
www.yini.org.uk

WEBSITES

www.ncwe.com
National Centre for Work Experience

www.graduatecareersonline.com/s4b
Specialised work experience project for students providing advice on finding work experience, as well as details of relevant work experience schemes and sources of vacancies.

www.tcsonline.org.uk
Teaching Company Scheme – a government-funded scheme that matches graduates with employment opportunities.

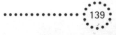

12. Appendices

Appendix A

THE RUSSELL GROUP OF UNIVERSITIES

This is an informal, self-selected, representative body of research-led universities, often held up as the elite. It is so called because meetings take place in the Russell Hotel.

The group comprises:

Birmingham
Bristol
Cambridge
Cardiff
University College London
Edinburgh
Glasgow
Imperial College London
Kings College London
Leeds
Liverpool
London School of Economics
Manchester
Newcastle upon Tyne
Nottingham
Oxford
Sheffield
Southampton
Warwick

Appendix B

INSTITUTIONS INCLUDED IN OUR SURVEY

Aberdeen
Abertay Dundee
University of Wales Aberystwyth
Anglia Polytechnic University
Aston
Bangor, University of Wales
Bath
Queen's University Belfast
Birmingham
Bournemouth
Bradford
Brighton
Bristol
Brunel
Buckingham
Cambridge
University of Wales Cardiff
Central England
Central Lancashire
City
Coventry
De Montfort
Derby
Dundee
Durham
East Anglia
East London
Edinburgh
Essex
Exeter
Glamorgan
Glasgow
Glasgow Caledonian
Goldsmith College London
Greenwich
Heriot-Watt
Hertfordshire
Huddersfield
Hull
Imperial College London
Keele
Kent
Kings College London

Kingston
University of Wales Lampeter
Lancaster
Leeds
Leeds Metropolitan
Leicester
Lincoln
Liverpool
Liverpool John Moores
London Guildhall
London School of Economics
Loughborough
Luton
Manchester
Manchester Metropolitan
Middlesex
Napier
Newcastle upon Tyne
North London
Northumbria
Nottingham
Nottingham Trent
Oxford
Oxford Brookes
Paisley
Plymouth
Portsmouth
Queen Mary & Westfield College London
Reading
Robert Gordon
Royal Holloway
St Andrews
Salford
Sheffield
Sheffield Hallam
Southampton
South Bank
Staffordshire
Stirling
Strathclyde
Sunderland
Surrey
Sussex

University of Wales Swansea
Teesside
Thames Valley
Ulster
UMIST
University College London

Warwick
Westminster
West of England
Wolverhampton
York

Appendix C

SOME SURVEY CONTRIBUTORS 1998–2002

This is not a comprehensive list of contributing recruiters. Those that expressed a wish to remain anonymous are not included.

A5 Direct; Watford
Abbey National; Milton Keynes
Acorn Recruitment & Training; Cardiff
Allen, Gordon & Co; Perth
Alliance & Leicester; Leicester
Alphametrics; Royston
Andersen Consulting (Accenture); London
Anglian Water Services; Huntingdon
Ascom Telecommunications; Cardiff
Astra Zeneca; Macclesfield
Audit Commission; Bristol
Avery Dennison; Maidenhead
Avon & Somerset Constabulary; Bristol
AXA Assurance; Coventry
BA Swallow Business Systems; London
Bacon & Woodrow; Epsom
Ballast Wiltshier; Winchester
Bank of England; London
Bank of Scotland; Edinburgh
Barber Harrison & Platt; Sheffield
Barnett Waddingham; London
BDO Stoy Hayward; London
Beever & Struthers; Manchester
BICC General UK Cables; Helsby
Blagden Chemicals; Haverhill
BMW Group UK; Warwick
Bucknall Austin; Birmingham
Bullimores Chartered Accountants; Dorking
Burges Salmon; Bristol
Bywater; Reading
Cambridge Pharma Consultancy; Cambridge
Canvas Holidays; Dunfermline
Carlbro Group; Peterborough
Center Piper Associates; Carshalton
City Logistics; Milton Keynes
Clement Keyes; West Bromwich
Coexis; Rickmansworth
Computacenter; Hatfield
Consignia; London
Cooper, GD & Co; Croydon
Crouch Chapman; London

CRU International; London
Delcam; Birmingham
Delta; West Bromwich
Druid Systems; Staines
Ecolochem International; Peterborough
Edmund Nuthall; Camberley
EDS; Uxbridge
ESDU; London
Fashion Personnel; London
FKI; Loughborough
Fluor Limited; Camberley
Ford Credit; Brentwood
Franklin & Andrews; London
Galliford; Hinckley
Games Workshop; Nottingham
Gardline Surveys; Great Yarmouth
GCHQ; Cheltenham
GEC; Chelmsford
Gestetner Management; London
Government Statistical Service; London
Grampian Country Food; Aberdeen
Grant Thornton; Coventry
Harris & Sutherland; London
Hays Montrose; London
HBG Construction; London
Henley College; Coventry
Hill Samuel Asset Management; London
HLB Kidsons; London
Holman Fenwick & Willan; London
Horwath Pulleyn Heselton; York
Hoyer UK; Huddersfield
HSBC Bank; London
Hunt Associates, Anthony; Cirencester
IMI; Birmingham
Independent Insurance; Edenbridge
Intelligent Applications; Livingstone
JDR CableSystems; Ely
Keane; Birmingham
Kerry Foods; Egham
Kingfisher; London
Kingston Smith; London
Larking Gowen; Norwich
Leonard Stace; Epping
Linguaphone Institute; London
Linklaters & Paines; London
Logica; London
Meteorological Office, The; London

Miller Civil Engineering; Rugby
Montgomery Watson; High Wycombe
Moore Stephens; Coleraine
Morton Thornton; St Albans
National Audit Office; London
Norwich Union; Norwich
Objective Professional Services; Reading
Padley, GW; Grantham
Parsons Energy & Chemicals; Brentford
Peel & Fowler; Birmingham
Perkins Engines Co; Peterborough
Peters Elworthy & Moore; Cambridge
Peugeot Motor Co; Coventry
PricewaterhouseCoopers; London
Produce Studies; Newbury
Promotional Campaigns Group; Keston
Quest Consulting; Aberdeen
Railtrack; London
Rainbow Gillespie; Newcastle upon Tyne
Raychem; Swindon
RHS Harntec; Exeter
Riverstone Management; Brighton
Ryecroft Glenton; Newcastle upon Tyne
Sanofi Pharmaceuticals; Guildford
Science Recruitment Group; Slough
Scorex (UK); Bradford
Scottish Equitable; Edinburgh
Sema Group; London
Shepway District Council; Folkestone
Silentnight Beds; Barnoldswick
Simoco Europe; Cambridge
Smart421; Welwyn Garden City
Snell & Willcox; Petersfield
Spirit Health & Fitness; London
ST Microelectronics; Bristol
Standard Life; Edinburgh
Stevens Company, The; London
Success Appointments; London
Synopsys; London
Syseca; Manchester
Torgersens; Sunderland
Towers Perrin; London
TRW ASG (UK); Birmingham
UCB Film; Wigton
UK Overseas Handling; London
United Biscuits; West Drayton
Ventham, MJ & Co; Rochford

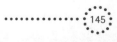

Vickers Defence Systems; Newcastle upon Tyne
Vodafone; Newbury
Voluntary Service Overseas; London
VSW; Macclesfield
Walker; Aylesbury
Walkers Snacks; Reading
Watts Gregory; Cardiff
Western Geophysical; London
White Waghorn; Stevenage
William M Mercer; London
Wincanton Logistics; Wincanton
Zonal Retail Data Systems; Edinburgh

Appendix D

PARTICIPANTS AND RECRUITS: BACKGROUND TO THE SURVEY DATA

The results presented in the latter part of this book are based on data collected between 1999 and 2001. The following tables provide some background to the recruiters participating in the survey during this time as well as their recruitment patterns.

TABLE 12.1 PROPORTION OF PARTICIPATING RECRUITERS ACTIVELY RECRUITING GRADUATES IN THE SURVEY YEAR

Actively recruiting	%
Yes	91.2
No	5.8
Not stated	3.1
TOTAL	100.1

TABLE 12.2 SIZE OF PARTICIPATING RECRUITERS

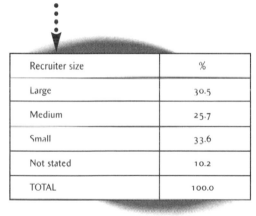

Recruiter size	%
Large	30.5
Medium	25.7
Small	33.6
Not stated	10.2
TOTAL	100.0

NOTE We have arbitrarily defined a large recruiter as one planning on recruiting 21 or more graduates this year; medium 8–20 graduates; and small 7 or less. These numbers have been chosen to generate roughly equal samples for each size.

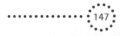

TABLE 12.3 LOCATION OF PARTICIPATING RECRUITERS

Recruiter location	%
North	11.1
Midlands	19.0
South	34.5
London	19.9
Scotland	7.5
Wales	1.3
Not stated	6.6
TOTAL	100.0

TABLE 12.4 GENDER OF PARTICIPATING RECRUITERS

Recruiter gender	%
Male	28.8
Female	48.2
Not stated	23.0
TOTAL	100.0

TABLE 12.5 PARTICIPATING RECRUITERS' PREDICTED GRADUATE
INTAKE, BY SUBJECT AREA

Subject areas	% of total recruitment
Business & Management	14.5
Civil Engineering/Construction	3.0
Computing/IT	14.1
Electrical Engineering/Electronics	7.7
Finance/Accountancy/Banking	4.8
General/Other Engineering	5.1
Languages	2.5
Law	5.1
Mathematics & Statistics	13.3
Science	6.8
Social Science/Economics	2.3
Other	10.5
Any/not known	10.1
TOTAL	100.0

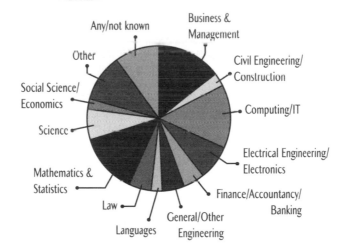

TABLE 12.6 PARTICIPATING RECRUITERS ACTIVELY RECRUITING IN THE SURVEY YEAR, BY SUBJECT AREA

Active recruiters by subject areas	% of total recruiters
Business & Management	13.5
Civil Engineering/Construction	7.4
Computing/IT	14.9
Electrical Engineering/Electronics	10.8
Finance/Accountancy/Banking	11.7
General/Other Engineering	10.1
Languages	5.2
Law	2.3
Mathematics & Statistics	9.5
Science	10.6
Social Science/Economics	4.1
TOTAL	100.0

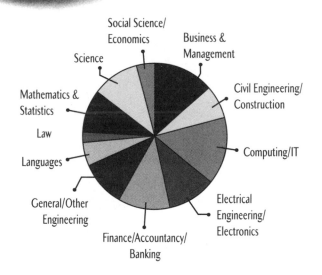

Appendix E

REFERENCE COURSES USED FOR VALUE-ADDED CALCULATIONS

Business & Management: N120 Business Studies
Civil Engineering/Construction: H200 Civil Engineering
Computing/IT: G500 Computing
Electrical Engineering/Electronics: H600 Electronic Engineering
Finance/Accountancy/Banking: N400 Accountancy
General/Other Engineering: H100 General Engineering
Languages: R100 French
Law: M300 Law
Mathematics & Statistics: G100 Mathematics
Science: F100 Chemistry
Social Science/Economics: L100 Economics

Appendix F

NOTES AND WARNINGS

Survey and participants

- The classification of organisations by region and size is arbitrary

- With consent, the names and locations in Appendix C are as stated on returns

- *We cannot claim the participants are fully typical*

- The questionnaire might change between or during surveys

- Our surveys do not enquire about many excellent providers of higher education. Their omission does *not* indicate lack of quality

- Bear in mind that many of the institutions in the results may have particular expertise in subjects not surveyed here (e.g. medicine, education, art and design)

- Results are from the last three surveys – 1999, 2000 and 2001.

Preferences for employability qualities

- The percentage figures given are the number of recruiters selecting the option as a percentage of all respondents

- Not all qualities were included in all three recent surveys.

Nominations

- Votes for institutions from participating recruiters are *not* our views

- They might not indicate quality, lack of it, or provision of a subject/service

- We report *all* votes, including multiple votes, anonymous returns, and votes not conforming to our understanding of provision

- Results are from the last three surveys – 1999, 2000 and 2001

- Rankings are particularly sensitive to fluctuation if a university's points score is close to zero

- Universities receiving no votes (positive or negative) are *not ranked*

- One employability point is awarded per vote (positive or negative); two points are awarded for votes coming from a respondent actively recruiting in that subject

- Universities are ranked according to (i) total employability points; (ii) vote difference; (iii) fewest negative votes

- 1998 rankings are based on the three annual surveys to 1998

- Due to minor adjustments (e.g. late inclusions, changes of subject categories, exclusion through double counting or company closure) some older data might not match with the previously published results.

Value-added

- Expected entry requirements are taken from *University and College Entrance: The Official Guide 2001 Entry* (aka the *Big Guide*) published by UCAS

- The expected entry requirements used are therefore a couple of years old. This should not impact on our results as such requirements tend not to change over short periods of time

- The expected entry requirements used in calculating value-added are expressed in terms of the *old* UCAS A-level points tariff. This is because many institutions are yet to adopt the new tariff (introduced in 2001) when providing offer information. Future reports will encompass the new tariff as its use becomes more widespread

- *Value-added is based on expected entry requirements for one particular reference course only*

- Reference courses are chosen as typical courses that are provided by many universities

- Reference courses are listed as Appendix E

- *Actual entrance offers are based on more than UCAS points alone.*

Comments and quotes

- Our comments and observations represent *only* what has caught our eye and are not meant to be taken as the last word. You should draw your own conclusions

- All quotes are taken directly from recruiters' responses

- If a recruiter singles out an institution for praise or criticism but doesn't provide a specific justification for their choice, it is taken to mean *'particularly good'* or *'unlikely to recruit from . . .'* respectively

- Some quotes are taken from the results of earlier surveys if particularly relevant.

More information can be found on our companion website:

- www.careers-portal.co.uk/earning